Kings & Queens

Kings & Queens

A History of British Monarchy

Ronald Pearsall

TODTRI

Introduction

The throne of the United Kingdom has been occupied – apart from a brief period in the seventeenth century – for more than a thousand years. The monarchy as an institution has survived wars, invasions, rebellions and economic disasters, and the history of the British Isles is inextricably linked with the lives of the kings and queens who have reigned over them. The fascinating personal chronology is also a revealing insight into the development of the constitutional role of the monarchy, from the early warrior kings of the pre-Conquest Heptarchy to today's royal family, whose members are, through television and newspapers, brought almost daily into their subjects' homes and put under closer scrutiny than seemed possible just a few years ago.

Every man and woman who has ascended the throne has left a mark, for good or ill, on the nation's life and development. This chronological account of their lives reveals just how great and how little their effect on the lives of their subjects and on the country has been. From Egbert to Elizabeth II, here is the complete story of their achievements and failures, their scheming and intrigues, their victories and defeats.

The first kings were provincial warlords, the most powerful being those of Wessex and Mercia, and they strove to establish a fragile supremacy over their rivals and each other. Egbert was the first to be accepted, albeit reluctantly, as all-powerful ruler. The insecurity of the hereditary principle meant that monarchs were always conscious of pretenders, real or imagined, to the throne, and close relatives lived in constant fear for their lives. Loyalties of kinship were often less important than the realities of holding on to power, and the history of the kings and queens of England is not especially pretty. Cold-blooded murder and internecine war weave their way through almost a thousand years, and it is not until the Hanoverians ascended the throne in the early eighteenth century that a settled pattern began to emerge and the principle of heredity through primogeniture became firmly established. At the same time, the pattern began to emerge of a largely benevolent monarch who interfered little in affairs of state and whose powers were circumscribed by a powerful parliament.

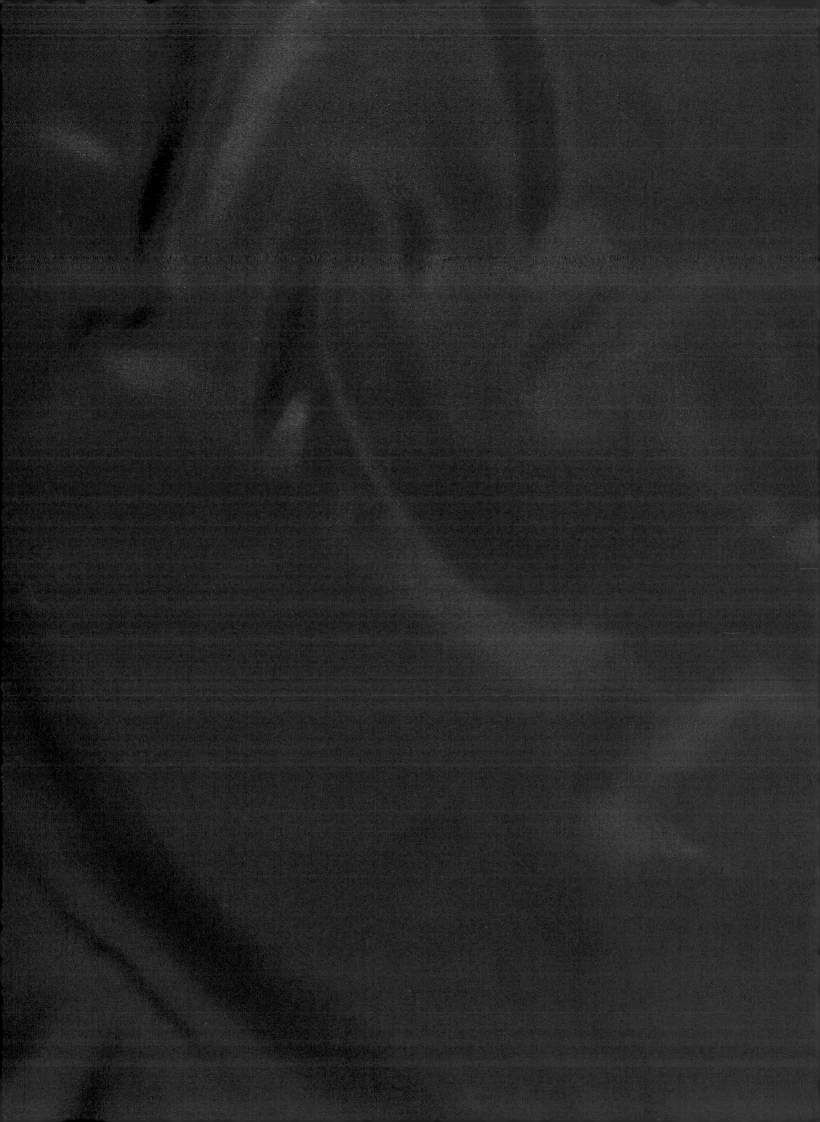

West Saxon Kings

By 613 the threat from the native Celts was believed to be
ended. England was divided into seven Anglo-Saxon king-
doms – Kent, Sussex, Essex, East Anglia, Wessex, Mercia
and Northumbria – known collectively as the Heptarchy, and each
of the seven kings strove for supremacy, while at the same time
trying to stave off the Vikings.

The Anglo-Saxons were themselves one-time invaders; they were
sophisticated, yet warlike. How sophisticated they were we know
from the excavation that took place in 1939 at Sutton Hoo,
Suffolk, of the burial ship of Rædwald, king of East Anglia
(*c*.600–617). The archaeologists uncovered armour, jewellery, coins
and silver of the highest quality and refinement.

THE COMING OF CHRISTIANITY

The seventh century was the darkest of the Dark Ages, though Christianity was taking root. In ninety years (597–686) conversion from ancestral heathenism was complete. In a few years England was the pride of western Christendom, and sent missionaries to convert the pagan Germans. Spiritual unity was not matched by political unity.

EGBERT (802–39)

At various times the minor kings occupied a neighbour's territory, but it was not until 827 that Egbert, king of Wessex, was acknowledged as king of all England. The son of Ealhmund, king of Kent, he made a premature bid for a vacant throne and was forced to flee, finding sanctuary at the court of Charlemagne, the most powerful monarch of Europe, a man who spoke both Greek and Latin, who sponsored the arts, agriculture and commerce, but who ruled his vassal states with ruthless efficiency. Egbert returned in 802 to fill the throne of Wessex.

For the first twelve years he reigned in relative peace, but then followed a war against Cornwall, where the Celts still held sway. Wessex's chief rival was Mercia. Mercia's king, Offa (757–96), had built a great defensive dyke between Wales and England (now known as Offa's Dyke) and in 794 had signed an agreement with Charlemagne to improve trade between Europe and England. By the time Egbert became king of Wessex, however, Mercia was in decline. It was mostly an inland area, while Wessex, stretching from Kent in the east to Cornwall in the west, had an enormous coastline, advantageous for overseas trade.

Egbert decisively defeated Mercia at the battle of Ellandun, Wiltshire, in 825. In 835 he was himself beaten by Scandinavian pirates at a battle in Dorset, although in 836 he defeated a Danish force at Hengestdune (Hingston Down) near the borders of Devon and Cornwall. The Danes had help from the Cornish, who had yet to be subdued.

The warring kings of England had little effect on the day-to-day life of the people. Armies were small, battles were short-term engagements, weapons were fairly primitive, and enemies could become allies overnight. Desirable as it was to get the better of a neighbouring king, the threat of the Vikings drove them together when danger threatened.

The Vikings had been a seafaring, piratical race since the days of the Romans, but since the fifth century they had restricted their activities to their own shores. Their sudden spates of attacks on England has long been a puzzle, but most probably the cause was Charlemagne's incursion into Denmark, which threatened the independence of the northern nations. In terror and resentment, the Vikings hit at the outer bastions of Christendom – England was ideally situated.

The Vikings' bellicose behaviour, at first practised by a minority, was so successful and profitable that the entire manhood of Denmark and Norway took to the pirate life. With utter control of the sea they could strike, pillage and loot, withdraw when any major force appeared and attack elsewhere.

Left: The first twelve years of Egbert's reign were relatively peaceful. But then he became involved in drawn out wars against Cornwall and Mercia. Such wars, however, had little effect on the everyday life of the general population.

EGBERT.
*Roy d'Angleterre,
en 801. Mort en 837.*

Above: Æthelwulf was a weak and kindly king, though in 851 he slaughtered an entire Danish army.

ÆTHELWULF (839–58)

Egbert died in 839, and his place was taken by his son Æthelwulf (Ethelwolf). Apparently a weak and kindly man, in 851 at "Aclea" (Oakley, south of the River Thames) he exterminated a whole Danish army: "the greatest slaughter among the heathen host that had been heard of down to that day." He was succeeded by his sons Æthelbald (Ethelbald; 858–60) and Æthelbert (Ethelbert; 860–65), who were shadowy, short-lived and incompetent. Æthelred I (Ethelred; 866–71), a third son, had more substance, fighting the Danes in six bloody pitched battles, but he was killed by the Danes in 871 at the battle of Ashdown, Berkshire.

ALFRED (871–99)

Æthelred I had left two young sons, but the men of Wessex needed a grown man to lead them and they turned to Æthelred's brother, one of the best known monarchs of all history, Alfred the Great (b.c.848). Much of Alfred's

ftir Egbrightht regned
his sone Ethelwolf opt
wyse clepid adolf And
held a parlement at Cirencester And
thedir come al the kinges of Eng

early reign was spent in keeping the continental hordes at bay, and in despair he even offered the Vikings money to go away, which gave him a breathing space. He reformed and rationalized the law and promoted the production of a history of the people of England, the *Anglo-Saxon Chronicle*. He was the first monarch who actually saw further than the next battle. He began to build a fleet of galleys and "long boats", crewed by renegade Vikings, and sought to establish a professional army.

He was religious without being bigoted, was generous to the enemies he defeated and looked for a consensus, willing to confer when necessary. He routed the Vikings at Ethandune in Wessex (Edington, Wiltshire) in 878, and signed the treaty of Wedmore, so that north of a line running roughly from London to Chester was the Danelaw, in which Danes could remain in their settlements and be treated as equals of the English before the law. The famous story of him allowing the cakes to burn took place shortly before this battle, when Alfred had taken refuge on the Isle of Athelney, Somerset, after a shock Danish attack.

Opposite: King Æthelwulf kneeling before the Pope in 855, attended by cardinals.

Left: Alfred the Great, an interpretation from the coins and busts that exist from the time.

The treaty of Wedmore may have satisfied those Danes who had settled in the north of England (surprisingly they kept to their side of the agreement), but there were more to come, and Alfred had to capture and rebuild London in 886. It was only now that the minor kings fully, but reluctantly, recognized him as king of England. England was still in a state of flux, with the Vikings settled comfortably and seemingly for ever inside the old Roman walls of York. In 882 Alfred reconstructed his navy, and his warships were twice the size of those of his adversaries. But the attacks still came.

Harry Payne

EDWARD THE ELDER (C.899–924)

Alfred died *c.*899, and he was succeeded by his son Edward the Elder (b.*c.*870). Edward continued the consolidation of his state, absorbing the Viking settlers until they became thoroughly English and giving them many important posts. He also obliged the Welsh to acknowledge him as their overlord, while his son, Athelstan (924–39), subdued the obdurate Northumbria and is best remembered for a great victory at Brunanburh, Cumbria, in 937 where he defeated a confederacy of almost everybody – Danes, Scots and Irish.

Opposite: Alfred's galleys in a battle with the Vikings. He was the first English monarch to appreciate the need for a formidable navy.

Left: Edward the Elder, who succeeded his father Alfred the Great who died in 899.

Below: Edmund I (939-946) ruled for only seven years, but tried to carry on the traditions of Alfred the Great.

EDMUND I (939–46)

In 939 Athelstan's brother, Edmund (b.921), succeeded him. He was a monarch who carried on Alfred's tradition, although he ruled for only seven years.

The lack of a leader of the calibre of Alfred the Great had increased the possibilities of one of the Viking settlers in the north making a move. Erick Haraldsson, known as Bloodaxe (d.954), had been king of Norway but had been expelled in 947 for his grotesque cruelty – it is alleged that he killed his seven brothers, a crime heinous even in Viking eyes. Erick took refuge in England and was accepted as king of Northumbria. He was ejected by Edmund's brother and successor, Eadred I (946–55), in 949, but returned to regain his crown. This time he was killed by Eadred at the battle of Stainmore, Yorkshire, and Northumbria, which had become an enclave of Viking rule, lost its independence. On his death in 955, Eadred was succeeded by his nephew, Eadwig (955–59).

It might seem that the Vikings were pursuing a vendetta against Britain, but their wrath was turned to the south as well. At the same time as their incursions against the English, they were rampaging through the continent of Europe. Charlemagne had beaten them, but his son, Louis I, known as the Pious (814–40), lacked his mettle, and the Vikings were surprised by the

ease with which they raped and plundered their way through France, the Low Countries and northern Germany, meeting little effective resistance save when the kings and nobles temporarily halted their dynastic and civil wars to deal with the marauders. In 885–86 30,000 Vikings, a colossal army for the period, besieged Paris and eventually had to be bought off when the French monarch, Charles the Fat, not only paid a huge ransom but allowed the Vikings to ravage Burgundy without his interference or condemnation.

Why did the Vikings triumph? Their military tactics were crude compared with those of the Romans. Although the use of the bow and arrow was known, their basic weapons were the sword, spear and the axe. Defensive armour consisted of a helmet, round shield and leather jacket, later replaced by the mail shirt. They had a high standard of discipline, and their opponents were often ill-trained and reluctant militia. The Vikings were eventually countered by professional cavalrymen who were able to harass the slow-moving Viking infantry; the Vikings learned. They adopted cavalry as well.

EDGAR (959–75)

In 959 Edgar the Peaceable (*Rex Pacificus*) attained the throne. For some reason, Viking raids subsided at this period, and Edgar, who was an enlightened king, undertook many reforms, including the issuing of a code of laws that strengthened the Anglo-Saxon system devised by Alfred the Great. He also divided the shires into what were known as hundreds. A new form of coronation ceremony was devised by St Dunstan, whom Edgar appointed as Archbishop of Canterbury c.959. Dunstan was a great man, a leader in repressing evil-living clergy and a valued statesman.

Above: Edgar was an enlightened king, strengthening the system of Anglo-Saxon law established by Alfred the Great.

Right: Edward the Martyr was only king for three years before being murdered by agents of his stepmother.

EDWARD (975–78)

In 975 Edgar died, only thirty-three years old, and Edward the Martyr became king. He was called the Martyr because he had reigned for just three years before being murdered by the agents of his stepmother who wished to promote her son Æthelred, Edward's half-brother.

The assassination of Edward the Martyr, making way for Æthelred the Unready, the first truly evil English king.

THE KING'S INCOME

The King derived his income from a wide variety of sources. There were the royal estates scattered throughout the country, there was his "farm", a food-rent paid to him by all the lands in his realm, sometimes in ale, corn, malt, honey dairy produce, and livestock.

There was also income from subject Kings, inheritances, tolls, and fines and forfeitures incurred in the law courts. He had many rights he could claim from almost anybody, and for a monetary consideration these rights could be exempted. In 855 a bishop of Worcester paid three hundred shillings to get his estate freed from the duty of feeding hawks, falcons, huntsmen and lords of the king.

Æthelred II, who alternately bribed invaders to go away or massacred those who had integrated with the Anglo-Saxons.

ETHELRED II. 979–1016.

ÆTHELRED II (978–1016)

Æthelred (Ethelred), known as the Unready, was the first, but by no means the last, wholly ineffectual king of England. Unready in this context means "redeless", void of foresight or lacking counsel. The Vikings renewed their attacks on England, the first serious invasion occurring in 991. The invaders were bribed to go away by the payment of Danegeld. They obliged briefly, but soon returned, and in 994 London was besieged by the army of Sweyn I, Forkbeard, king of Denmark (986–1014). The citizens managed to beat off the Danes, but the invaders pillaged the southeast of England before the payment of further Danegeld encouraged them to withdraw.

In 1002 Æthelred over-reached himself – he ordered the massacre of St Brice's Day, during which many Danes living in England, many of whom had been assimilated into the population, were put to death. Among those massacred was the sister of Sweyn. The subsequent Danish invasion of England met with little resistance, perhaps because the English decided that enough was enough and no one could be worse than Æthelred. Although Æthelred built a fleet to repel any further incursions, he was eventually forced to flee to Normandy, returning the year after when Sweyn died. Sweyn's son, Cnut (Knut or Canute), attempted to assume power, but was driven out, although not before cutting off the hands, ears and noses of English hostages he had taken.

ANGLO-SAXON MEDICINE

Anglo-Saxon medicine was a mixture of magic and folk remedies. The Holy Salve, a dressing for wounds, was made from sixty named herbs, of which the largest proportions were of lovage, parsley, and groundsel. The herbs were mixed with butter. Some medical knowledge, based on Greek and Arabian medicine, filtered through to England, via Salerno in Italy, the medical centre of Europe. "Arabian" medicine was not necessarily Moslem; Arabic was the language the information was conveyed in. The enemy of medical research was the church, which refused to allow bodies to be dissected for research on account of the belief in the resurrection of the body. Some illnesses, such as leprosy, became a crime. The ancestor of biochemistry was uroscopy, the examination of the urine. It was believed by the Arabs that the sex of an unborn child could be determined by an examination of the mother's urine. The presence of blood bile, or a heavy sediment, it was later realized, indicated the nature of an ailment.

Danish Kings

The Danish dynasty was brief. It might seem that Alfred the Great had failed. But had he? His ancestors had been invaders too, and he had more in common with the Danes than the inhabitants of the far-flung reaches of his kingdom. The conquest of England by William of Normandy was inevitable when Edward the Confessor became king; he had lived in Normandy for twenty-five years, and was in sympathy with Norman aspirations.

Above: Cnut was monarch of all England, which became part of an empire encompassing Norway, Denmark and southern Sweden.

CNUT (1016–35)

Two years later, in 1016, Æthelred died, and England was faced by two contenders for the throne, Edmund Ironside, the son of Æthelred, and Cnut, the son of Sweyn. The succession could be decided only by conflict, and at the battle of Ashingdon in Essex Cnut defeated Edmund. They agreed to divide the country in two, Cnut taking the north and Edmund the south. This was a short-lived arrangement, however, because Edmund, who had reigned as Edmund II, suddenly died, and Cnut became monarch of all England, which became part of an empire encompassing Norway, Denmark and southern Sweden.

At first it seemed that Cnut would be as harsh a ruler as the Vikings' reputation suggested, and he was at first every bit as vicious as Æthelred, putting to death the most powerful English chiefs, exiling Edmund's two young sons and levying harsh taxes. However, once he had established his authority, Cnut proved as conciliatory, efficient and benevolent as Alfred. He replaced the Danish nobles by English earls, showed reverence for the church and ushered in a new age of enlightenment and prosperity.

Right: King Cnut is widely reputed to have ordered the waves to stop, but he was actually proving to his sycophantic courtiers that even kings could not control nature. He proved to be a good king after his early excesses, doing much to reconcile the Anglo-Saxons and the Danes.

Harold Harefoot reigned from 1035 to 1040, a cruel and reckless monarch who did much to undo the good work of many of his predecessors.

HAROLD I (1035–40)

Cnut had married Æthelred's widow, Emma, in 1017, so there was a sense of continuity when he died, illusory though it proved to be. The rightful heir, Harthacnut (the son of Cnut and Emma), had to give way to Harold I, known as Harold Harefoot (the son of Cnut and his English mistress Ælgifu), although Harthacnut gained the throne when Harold Harefoot died. Harold Harefoot ruled with cruelty and reckless abandon, and Harthacnut, who ruled for only two years (1040–42), did not have time to make amends.

A disturbing pattern was emerging, perhaps inescapable with hereditary monarchy: a good ruler was often followed by a poor ruler, who would turn back the clock. Progress of sorts was made, however, for the actions of kings did not greatly affect the lives of the mass of the people. Far more important to them were the earls, the local overlords, who could take their lead from the king or who could pursue their own paths, good or bad. There was a medley of races and a mix of languages. The people muddled on. England as a coherent state was still not in being, although already in existence were the elements of feudalism, the social system by which the lower orders of society served the middle orders and the middle orders served the higher.

Edward the Confessor ascended the throne in 1042, having spent much of his life in Normandy with his mother. Wise and strong, he sponsored the Norman way of life and promised the crown to William of Normandy in 1051.

EDWARD THE CONFESSOR (1042–66)

Waiting in the wings during the reigns of Harold I and Harthacnut was Edward the Confessor, the son of Æthelred the Unready and Emma. Edward was born *c.*1003, but he had lived in Normandy with his mother from the age of ten until he was thirty-five years old. Pious, wise and strong, he ascended the throne in 1042 after the death of Harthacnut, although Harthacnut had invited him to his court a year earlier.

In an attempt to restrict the power of the restless earls, he tended to sponsor Norman nobles rather than the native English. His long years among the Normans, who were originally Vikings who had settled in northwest France in the early tenth century, had led him to view Norman culture as inherently superior to that of the Anglo-Saxons, and in a move that paved

Edward the Confessor at a banquet. The inscription is in Norman French, a sign of the great changes ahead.

the way for a new dynasty, he promised the English throne to William of Normandy in 1051.

The Vikings were nearing the end of their troublesome incursions, but Edward had to deal with Godwin, earl of Wessex, and his son Harold, who tried to sever Edward's links with Normandy. Edward married Godwin's only daughter, Edith, in 1045, but, influenced by his Norman favourites, he forced Godwin into exile. In 1053 Edward changed his mind, and Godwin returned to England, where he became Edward's closest and most trusted adviser, with the result that Edward went back on his earlier undertaking and promised Godwin's son, Harold, the throne. After Godwin's death in 1053, Harold became Edward's chief adviser, handling the affairs of state with gentleness yet vigour. He was no stranger to battle, having successfully driven back the Welsh and adding Herefordshire to his earldom. He made a pilgrimage to Rome in 1058, reinforcing England's links with Europe, but his attitude towards William of Normandy was ambivalent. Nevertheless, it was widely assumed, at least in England, that Harold would become king.

HAROLD II (1066)

In 1064, after trouncing the Welsh once again and aware that there was trouble brewing in the north, Harold was shipwrecked off the coast of Normandy. He visited William of Normandy (probably under pressure) and assured him that he would support his claim to the throne. He also supplied troops to help William fight the Bretons. Yet when Edward died in 1066, Harold had no compunction about becoming king.

Harold's brother, Tostig, who had become earl of Northumbria in 1055, had been replaced, with Harold's help, by Morcar, but in 1066 Tostig had

Despite his promise to William of Normandy, Edward the Confessor also offered the crown to Harold II, who eagerly accepted, though he only reigned for a few months before being killed by William at the Battle of Hastings.

persuaded the king of Norway, Harald Hardrada, to help him try to regain his lands, and Vikings sailed up the River Humber. Their initial attempts were successful, and at the battle of Fulford they defeated the earls of Northumberland and Mercia. On 16 September 1066 Harold assembled an army and set out from London. On 25 September he achieved a great and bloody victory against Tostig and Harald Hardrada at Stamford Bridge, Yorkshire. Both Tostig and Harald were killed, and of the 300 Norwegian ships that had sailed for England only twenty-four returned.

On 28 September William of Normandy landed at Pevensey in Sussex. His army has been estimated at anything between 7,000 and 50,000, with one historian putting the figure at 20,000 infantrymen and 12,000 cavalry. Harold, with his army of about 9,000 men, marched south from Yorkshire, while William built fortifications. Knowing that the Norman army was larger and better trained, Harold decided to go on the defensive. Most of the

The death of Harold, a detail from the Bayeux Tapestry. The direction of the arrows is wrong; they were fired high to fall down on Harold's army.

army, twenty deep, was ranged on a ridge 400–500 yards (365–460 metres) long at Senlac (near where Battle is today), with the cavalry and the best of the troops at the highest point in the centre of the ridge.

The Norman army advanced in three lines soon after dawn; the front line included crossbowmen (the first recorded mention of this weapon) as well as longbowmen, with the second line of men with pikes, followed by the cavalry. The Norman archers, firing uphill, were ineffective, the pikemen were repelled, the cavalry was scattered. Amazed at his success, Harold and his army left their defensive positions, and William feigned flight. Harold fell into the trap. His army, mainly armed with swords, pikes and battle-axes, was severely mauled when the Norman cavalry counter-attacked. The archers were instructed to fire high so that the arrows fell on the opponents; when Harold was struck in the eye and killed, the battle of Hastings was over. It was the most momentous battle in the history of England.

House of Normandy

The throne had been promised to William the Conqueror, and, the greatest general in Europe he was not a man to be trifled with. His battle plans were superior to those of Harold, and his men were fresh. It was no contest. William gave lands to the Knights who had aided him; this was to cause trouble for centuries to come. The licence to build castles was a licence to rebel against any weakling who came to the throne.

Above: William granting land to his nephew, the Earl of Brittany. The disposition of England to Norman nobles was one of the reasons for the continuing tensions in England, tensions that were to last for centuries.

Opposite: A powerful interpretation of William the Conqueror, perhaps sixteenth century.

Below: The invasion of England by William of Normandy. Despite the small ships the army was believed to number 32,000, though some put the figure at no more than 7,000.

WILLIAM I (1066–87)

William occupied Dover, and although London rejected his demand for its surrender, William began to devastate the surrounding countryside with great cruelty, and submission followed. William was crowned king on Christmas Day 1066.

William was a vigorous and determined man. He had never lost a battle and was the foremost general in Europe. The population of England was easily subjugated, as were insurrections by Hereward the Wake, aided by Danes, and the earls of Hereford and Norfolk, among many others. If the Anglo-Saxon hierarchy felt itself ill-used – as indeed it was – it showed it. French provinces under William's rule that had sought independence while William was elsewhere were swiftly brought to heel.

William the Conqueror was physically strong, charismatic, patient, devout, yet ruthless and cruel. He had been accompanied to England by many French nobles, who were granted estates confiscated from the Anglo-Saxons, and who were licensed to build castles. The feudal system had begun. And so did systematic rule. No one knew what England consisted of, what its wealth amounted to, what the inhabitants did and why or how many there were of them. The Domesday Book, which listed everything, even the numbers of livestock, and which covered all England except the far north (still a dangerous area), was completed shortly before William's death. It was a magnificent achievement, considering that England was a land of forests and intractable wilderness. It was not done out of love of learning, but to find out who and what to tax.

William's legacy was immense. Canterbury Cathedral was rebuilt; the White Tower of the Tower of London was begun; Scotland was invaded and the king, Malcolm III, Canmore (1057–93), obliged to pay homage; the Pope was refused traditional homage; and the New Forest was enclosed as a royal hunting area. There has been some debate about whether William the Conqueror was a "Good Thing"; whether the culture represented by the Anglo-Saxons would have been preferable; and whether firm repression, eventually represented by 2,000 castles, is better than haphazard chaos.

The Conqueror died in 1087 when his horse stumbled as he was besieging the French city of Nantes. He left Normandy to Robert, his son, and England to William, his third son.

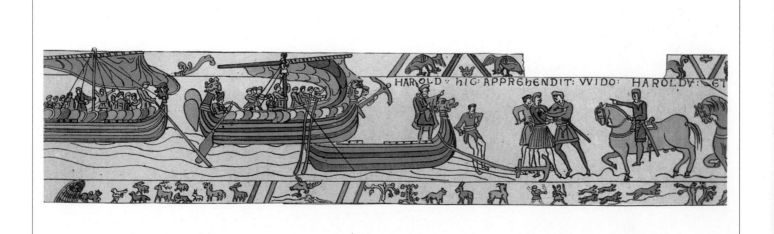

WILLIAM.   CONQVEROR.

MVSEVM
BRITAN
NICVM

Ego Willms cognoïe Bastard Rex Anglie do ¬
concedo tibi Nepoti meo Alano Brotamïe Coïti
¬ hredibs tuis inïptm oïes villas ¬ trař que
nuř fueřut Comitis Edwïni in Eboracsň
¬ cū feodis militū ¬ eccliš ¬ aliř libtat
Edwïni ita tenuit. ita libet honořifice sicut idé
Cuitate Ebor. Datū in obsidione corā

WILLIAM II (1087–1100)

William II (b.c.1056), called William Rufus because of his red complexion, was the Conqueror's third son. Although Robert had inherited Normandy, he wanted England as well, and there was continual warfare and hostility between the brothers. Many Norman nobles, given lands in England by the Conqueror, favoured Robert, but William II offered bribes in the form of a relaxation of forest laws and taxes to those who supported him, even though he betrayed the confidence of many of his followers. Nobles, in turn, betrayed the king, and many changed sides time and time again.

William II also pillaged the church revenues, and bishoprics and other high church posts were left unfilled so that the king could garner the revenues. Described as short and stout, intelligent, witty and generous to his soldiers, he had a pronounced stutter, never married and may have been a homosexual. He was killed, accidentally or not, by an arrow when hunting in the New Forest. His younger brother, Henry, was in the party at the time, and the royal treasury at Winchester (the target for any usurper) was removed by Henry the day after the fatality, so there may be grounds for the rumours that the death was not wholly accidental. Whatever the circumstances, many, especially men of the church, were glad to see the last of William Rufus.

Opposite: William presenting a charter to his nephew Alan. This time the annotation is in Latin, and there is no reluctance to call him William known as the Bastard (which was true).

Below: William II called Rufus because of his ruddy complexion, a monarch of ill-repute and untrustworthiness who pillaged church revenues and who was killed, accidentally or not, whilst hunting in the New Forest.

WILLIAM II (1087–1100)

Known as Beauclerc or the Scholar, Henry I as an old man - he died aged sixty-seven when this was an extraordinary age - is here given the heroic treatment.

HENRY I (1100–35)

Henry I (b.1068), known as Beauclerc or the Scholar, was the youngest son of William the Conqueror. He was a skilled administrator and a believer in legal reform. Although he had innumerable mistresses and illegitimate children, he kept on good terms with his wife Matilda (the Norman version of Eadgyth), a daughter of Malcolm III of Scotland, throughout the eighteen years of their marriage. Well-educated and placid, he could be astonishingly cruel and ruthless, but the reforms he sought to introduce to England were diluted by the continuing conflict with his brother, Robert of Normandy. Robert was finally defeated in 1106 and spent the last twenty-eight years of his life in prison.

Nevertheless, Henry I has an important place in English history. In 1110 the Pipe Rolls, official accounts records of sheriffs and other officials, were introduced, and these continued until 1834. In his reign, too, itinerant justices and the royal exchequer were established. More significant, in 1123 St Bartholomew's Hospital was founded in London. History consists of more than battles.

Henry I's only legitimate son, William, was drowned in 1120 when the White Ship, the vessel on which he was returning to England from Normandy, ran aground, the crew being drunk on wine he had supplied to them. Without a male heir, Henry persuaded the barons to accept his daughter, Matilda, as heir to the throne. Before he died of food poisoning near Rouen in France in 1135, Matilda (the widow of emperor Henry V) had married Geoffrey, count of Anjou (1113–51), thus reinforcing the continental drift of the monarchy.

EARLY HOSPITALS

St Bartholomew's Hospital, London, is the first known foundation by a private patron. It was started by a man named Rayer or Rahere (d.1144), a councillor to, or civil servant of, Henry I. It is said that on a visit to Rome on the king's business he suffered an attack of fever and was so impressed by St Bartholomew's hospital on the Tiber that he vowed to start a similar institution when he returned. St Bartholomew's was begun in 1123; in 1148 it was described as a special resort for "languishing men grieved with various sores". The foundation date of the earliest hospital in England is not known; the first authentic mention is a grant of land in 937 made by king Athelstan to an already established "Saxon hospital" in York. A hospital in Flixton-in-Holderness in Yorkshire (then part of Northumbria) was intended: "to preserve travellers from being devoured by the wolves and other voracious forest beasts."

The largest of the London hospitals was St Mary Spital, which was founded in 1197; it had accommodation for 180 sick poor. Long completely disappeared, it is remembered in the district name, Spitalfields.

Opposite: Henry I was a skilled administrator, anxious to reform the law, but any good he could do was dissipated by constant conflict with his brother Robert of Normandy.

HOUSE OF BLOIS

STEPHEN (1135–54)

While Henry I was alive, Stephen, William the Conqueror's grandson, had agreed that Matilda was to be the monarch, but on the king's death he seized the throne, with the support of the English barons, who likewise had no wish to see a woman on the throne.

Matilda invaded England in 1139 to claim the throne, and civil war broke out. Stephen also faced war with Matilda's uncle, king of Scotland, and in 1141 Stephen was taken prisoner.

But there was not to be a queen Matilda. Fiery and arrogant, she was betrayed, Stephen resumed control, and in 1148 Matilda retired from the fray, leaving the coming struggle to her son, Henry, who landed in England in 1153 and gathered support for war against Stephen. The battle of Wallingford of 1154 was indecisive.

Stephen's reign was meaningless. The barons, whom William the Conqueror had kept under control, showed that they could control events when it was in their interests to do so. The monarchy was marginalized, and the wealth of the country wasted in vainglorious expeditions in France. And no one anticipated any change when Henry II came to the throne.

House of Plantagenet

The Plantagenets began well with the most able king since Alfred the Great. Henry II broke the power of the barons by destroying their castles, and although the barons simmered they were obliged to await a weaker king.

They did not have to wait long. Richard I, the Lionheart, was an absentee king forever fighting, and after him came John, evasive and devious, easily out-witted by the barons and forced to sign the Magna Carta. Many future Plantagenets were in thrall to the barons; they could make or break kings at will, using parliament as a tool if needed. The last of the true Plantagenets, Richard II, died in Pontefract Castle, starved, and deprived of heat and clothing.

HENRY II (1154–89)

Henry II was the first of the Plantagenet kings. The name Plantagenet derives from *planta genista*, flowering broom, a nickname given to Henry II's father, Geoffrey, count of Anjou, although not formally used in a dynastic sense until the fifteenth century. The Plantagenets married among themselves, and there were strong family likenesses – a tendency to reddish hair, muscularity and strength, boistcrousness and courage – they were, in fact, rather too colourful for their own good. Henry married Eleanor of Aquitaine, the divorced wife of Louis VII of France, and established a dynasty that spanned thirteen Plantagenet kings over 331 years, although during the last eighty-six of those years, rival Plantagenet groups – the houses of Lancaster and the York – struggled to seize the crown.

Henry II was the strongest and most able king of England since Alfred, and during his reign England prospered. He dealt with the barons by destroying their castles, most of which were made of wood and earth, and replacing them with stone castles of his own. The barons simmered, but this was not another Stephen, and there was no contender lurking in the wings.

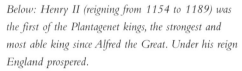

Below: Henry II (reigning from 1154 to 1189) was the first of the Plantagenet kings, the strongest and most able king since Alfred the Great. Under his reign England prospered.

Right: Matthew Paris (c1200 - 1259) was one of the greatest scholars of his time, author of Historia Major, a history of the world from the Creation. To be less than deferential was to court disaster, and the kings depicted (Henry II, Richard I, Henry III, and John) (reading clockwise) are shown with their architectural creations.

Sadly, all that most people know about Henry II was that he was indirectly responsible for the murder of Thomas à Becket.

During his ten year reign Richard I spent only seven months in England. Most of the time he was abroad fighting, and he is often pictured in a martial role.

Richard 1.ˢᵗ King of England and Earl of Anjou   *Duke of Normandy & Aqu... surnamed Coeur de Lion.*

against state interference, excommunicating those he thought were guilty of malpractice. Henry attempted to limit the secular powers of the clergy, especially the church courts, through the Constitutions of Clarendon, but Becket opposed the king, and in 1170 the archbishop was killed by four of Henry's knights in Canterbury Cathedral. They were Fitzurse, Tracy, Brito and Morville, who had overheard Henry's exasperated remark: "Of the cowards that eat my bread, is there none will rid me of this turbulent priest?"

Sadly, this is all most people know of Henry II. A year later Henry invaded Ireland, and was accepted as lord of Ireland; he was already lord of Wales, duke of Normandy, count of Anjou and ruler of Poitou, Brittany, Maine, Gascony and Aquitaine. His reign ended in disappointment and confusion, however. The Irish clergy submitted to Rome. And as early as 1173 Becket was canonized, Henry doing penance at his tomb in 1174. His sons Richard and Geoffrey fomented rebellion against him in 1173–4, and another son, John, was driven from Ireland. Henry died in France in 1189, at war with the French king. He had done much, but with his intellectual gifts he could have done more.

RICHARD I (1189–99)

Richard I, Cœur de Lion, the Lionheart (b.1157), was the third son of Henry II. He was everything expected from a king; tall, powerful, well-educated, musical and immensely courageous. He spoke little English, which did not matter much, because during his ten-year reign he spent only seven months in England. The rest of the time he was fighting abroad, especially in the Third Crusade (1189–92), one of the attempts to wrest Jerusalem from the hands of the Saracens. The Crusades were financed by heavy taxes, which were bitterly resented.

Richard was a brilliant commander, skilled in logistics and tactics; he even organized a laundry corps so that his soldiers had clean clothing. The armies he controlled numbered about 30,000, even though Philip II, king of France, joint leader with Richard, withdrew, at odds with the English king. Richard took Caesarea and Jaffa and although Jerusalem was not taken, Saladin, the leader of the Saracens (Turks), agreed to terms. On his return to Europe, Richard was captured by his enemy, the duke of Austria, who handed him over to Henry VI, emperor of Germany. A huge ransom was demanded for him, which was raised by means of an unpopular property tax and paid in part, but no sooner had he arrived back in England than he went off to fight again, this time in France, where he was mortally wounded.

During Richard's absences, England was initially run by William de Longchamp (d.1197), chancellor and joint justiciar. Although low-born, Longchamp was responsible for creating a form of bureaucracy, and thus one of the most useless kings was responsible, albeit indirectly, for laying down a governmental infrastructure that in some respects exists until our own time.

JOHN (1199–1216)

After Longchamp's death and while Richard was fighting in France, his youngest brother, John (b.1167), took command. He became king in 1199.

John speedily lost most of the French possessions in France (from which he received the nickname Lackland), was excommunicated by the pope for appropriating church property and antagonized the barons by his evasive-

Opposite: It is no wonder that Richard I was known as Lionheart. He was all that was expected of a king; and, as he was out of the country so much, capable administration could go ahead without royal hindrance.

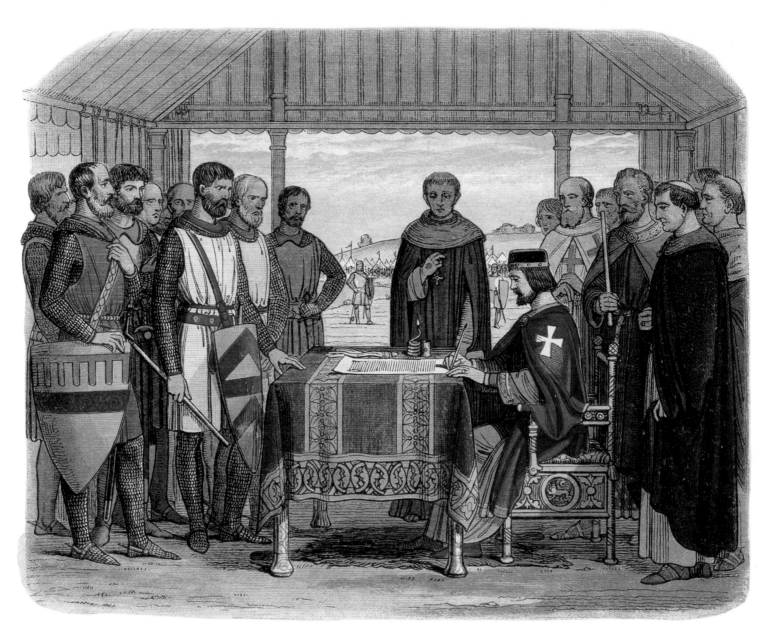

King John signing the Magna Carta in 1215. It is unlikely to have been the orderly ceremony seen here.

ness, unreliability and high levels of taxation. In 1215 at Runnymede near Windsor he was obliged to sign the Magna Carta (Great Charter), which limited his powers, especially in regard to the church and the nobility. Although much in the Magna Carta is petty, irrelevant and occasionally retrograde, parts of it were significant. It contained sixty-three clauses, which sought to curtail the power of the king to tax the barons (naturally), to guarantee church rights (unenforceable), to uphold the rights of city corporations (a sop to the increasing power of merchants and traders) and to make law more equitable. No free man could be arrested or imprisoned except by the judgement of his equals or by the law of the land: "to no man will we sell, or deny, or delay, right or justice."

The king was accused by the pope of not adhering to the clauses contained in the Charter, civil war broke out, the barons allied themselves with France and a French army captured the Tower of London. In the last year of his life king John lost his army; he also lost his cash and jewels in a sudden tide on the Wash in East Anglia while on campaign. Despite his poor reputation, in John's reign improvements in the administration of the exchequer,

*The Magna Carta was nowhere near as important as ı
might seem. Many of its doctrines were retrogressive. It
was a baron's charter, and John did not adhere to it.
Here he is depicted refusing to sign certain statutes.*

the law courts and civil administration were made. During his reign, too, the
old London Bridge was completed, a great feat of engineering and architecture – stone-built, with 140 shops, a drawbridge, a double row of houses, all
resting on nineteen arches.

*Above: Windsor Castle, the traditional home of the
monarch, has undergone many changes. Few centuries
have gone by without it being remoulded and refash-
ioned. This is how it appeared in 1887.*

HENRY III (1216–72)

John's eldest son was only nine years old when he gained the throne in
1216. During his minority the country was wisely governed by two regents,
but in 1227 Henry took over the reins himself. One of the regents died, and
the other was dismissed by Henry on a trumped-up charge of treason.
Fickle, petulant and more interested in the arts than war, he was easy prey
to the barons, led by the ambitious Simon de Montfort, earl of Leicester
(*c.*1208–65). Henry was obliged to sign the Provisions of Oxford, limiting
his powers and his habit of appointing family members and favourites to
key posts. Henry rapidly repudiated the agreement, and the Baron's War
broke out in 1264. Henry was defeated at the battle of Lewes, during which
Henry's son, Edward, was captured. The following year de Montfort sum-

Henry III, the oldest son of John, was nine when he became king, and the country was ruled by wise regents. Henry took over, and quickly roused the wrath of the barons by his petulance and instability. Despite this, the age was one of advance and progress.

moned the first English parliament, which consisted of lords, bishops, knights and burgesses (citizens) representing the towns. Parliamentary democracy? Such was not to be. The barons quarrelled among themselves, treachery was afoot, and de Montfort himself was killed by Edward at the battle of Evesham.

Despite all this, the age saw great advances in building, education and the arts. Oxford had three colleges; Cambridge University was founded in 1209; and fine writing and magnificent illuminated manuscripts poured from the monasteries. Westminster Abbey was improved, and cathedrals were built at Salisbury (1220–58) and Wells (1230–39), perhaps the supreme achievements of the century. Roger Bacon, the scientist, at Oxford from 1250 to 1257, made discoveries in optics and chemistry so penetrating that he was thought to be a magician. The machinations of king and barons in their quest for power pale into insignificance compared with these epoch-making events.

EDWARD I (1272–1307)

Henry III's son, who became Edward I (b.1239), was known as Longshanks because he was 6 feet (1.8 metres) tall; not a remarkable height now, but unusual and striking in those days. Capricious, bullying and endowed with a violent temper, Edward (b.1239) was a powerful and enlightened king, instituting the post of justice of the peace and controlling highway robbery and violence in the Statute of Winchester of 1285. Parliament was further strengthened. Democracy was a step nearer.

Needless to say, his energies were dissipated by wars, chiefly against Wales and Scotland. Wales was partly subdued, but Scotland proved more problem-

Opposite: The Coronation chair, depicted about 1860. The ceremonial has continually been altered, disregarding precedents, Christianising it, trying to bring it in line with a spurious English tradition.

Bel, and Jacques de Chastill[...]
nobleman engages to furnish h[...]
de fer, " a hundred suits of iron armo[...]

Above: An image of Edward II enshrined in an ornamental B of a Victorian book on armour. His companion is almost certainly Gaveston.

Gaveston did not last long. The nobles forced Edward to exile him. A year or two after his return he was kidnapped by the king's enemies and beheaded by the side of the road. Parliament, beginning to flex its muscles, set up a committee to control the king. Parliament was a child of the barons, and it needed a strong king to counter it. Edward II was not that man. An expedition against Scotland ended in failure, and Robert the Bruce defeated Edward at the battle of Bannockburn (1314), affirming Scottish independence.

The failure in Scotland was followed by uprisings in Wales and Ireland, but somehow, when the barons rose against the king, Edward, with his new favourite, Hugh le Despenser, managed a crushing victory at the battle of Boroughbridge in Yorkshire (1322).

Right: Edward II with Gaveston, by the historical painter Marcus Stone (1840 - 1921). For the Victorians, the relationship was shrouded in mystery. For generations of schoolchilden the pair were "chums".

It was a short-lived success for the beleaguered king. In 1326 his wife left him and, with her lover Roger Mortimer, seized power and deposed Edward, who was formally deposed by parliament in favour of his son, later Edward III. The king was imprisoned and put to death in Berkeley Castle in Gloucestershire. Isabella and Mortimer had insisted that there should be no marks of violence on him, and he was disembowelled – *cum vro ignito inter celanda confossus* (by means of a hot iron inserted into the rectum), the preferred death for homosexuals.

Increasingly, national wealth was irrelevant to the machinations of kings and nobles, although it is doubtful whether anyone questioned the viability of the institution of monarchy. Judgement on dissidents was quick, vicious and nasty. In 1316, for example, the citizens of Bristol rebelled and ejected the royal judges, and withstood a siege for a short while. It was a symptom of the time. Uprisings of the masses were inevitably crushed.

Above: The Battle of Crécy (1346) saw the annihilation of the French army which lost 10,000 men; the English lost 200. It was a taste of things to come and left France "a heap of ruins".

EDWARD III (1327–77)

Edward III came to the throne in 1327 at the age of fourteen. It was not an easy period, for his mother and her lover ignored the Regency Council and exercised power themselves. Edward took personal control in 1330, and in a demonstration of his sterner character, forced Isabella into retirement and had Mortimer tried and executed. He reigned for fifty years, an incredible achievement in an age when most people died before they were forty, and it would have been an age of greater prosperity had Edward not resumed hostilities with France, leading to the Hundred Years' War, which in the end profited no one.

Left: Edward III reigned for fifty years, a miraculous achievement when life expectancy was less than forty. The great disaster of his reign was the Black Death, in which a third of the population died.

Edward III with Guy of Flanders and a scribe. The barons lurked in the background, ready to strike when the time was right.

Edward achieved great victories. At Crécy (1346) the French lost 10,000 men, the English 200. French castles were endlessly besieged, treaties were made and broken, and ultimately France, bedevilled by civil war between two opposing royal factions, became, according to the Italian poet Petrarch, "a heap of ruins". However, just as important as Crécy, was the sea battle of Sluys (1340) in which an English fleet of 150 ships annihilated a French force of 190 ships; 166 French vessels were sunk or captured. England had command of the seas, and this ensured freedom of trade with the Low Countries. It was a short-lived freedom, however, for in 1372 a Franco-Spanish fleet defeated an English fleet.

Edward's reign saw the meteoric rise of the merchant class. Hitherto, coins had been silver, but in 1344 the golden noble (worth 6s 8d) was introduced. Many European trading nations followed the lead. The Black Death reached England in 1348 and the end of the following year had spread to the north of the country. It is estimated that at least 20 per cent of population died, and this led to the imposition in 1351 of the Statute of Labourers, which fixed wages at pre–Black Death levels and prevented mobility of labour in an attempt to restore stability at a time when demand for workers was much greater than the supply.   There was little trouble with the barons, although Scotland remained untamed. The Scottish king David II invaded England in 1346 but was defeated and captured.

Edward's eldest son, Edward, the Black Prince (1330–76), became a hero in his own right. Reckoned the greatest commander in Europe, he was at his best in the war against France, winning the battle of Poitiers (1356)

Opposite: The Order of the Garter, the oldest order of chivalry, being awarded to the Black Prince, Edward III's eldest son, and the brilliant commander of his army. The Black Prince died a year before his father; had he lived the history of the monarchy would have been greatly different.

largely through the skill of his archers, especially the longbowmen, and the courage of his infantry in hand-to-hand combat. The Black Prince did not follow up his success; had he done so he may have shortened the war. He also fought in Spain, but was mortally wounded while campaigning in France, and died a year before his father.

This was the age of chivalry, when qualities such as courtesy, bravery, honour and the protection of women were highly regarded. In 1348 Edward III founded the Most Noble Order of the Garter, echoing the ideals of king Arthur. Membership was restricted to twenty-four Knights, and its symbol was (and still is) a dark blue garter, worn below the left knee. The existing chapel of St Edward at Windsor Castle was converted for the Order's use. The word chivalry derives from chevalier, meaning knight, the embodiment of all chivalric ideals. The knight's armour was beautifully wrought, the wearer was mounted on a colossal horse, and tournaments or jousts, which had existed in some form or other from the ninth century, were designed to show the mounted knight at his best. It was a noble ideal. In reality the heavily protected knight could be knocked off his horse and killed by a sword-wielding ruffian. Loyalty could often be bought, and honour was in the eye of the beholder.

Edward III died of senile dementia in 1377. In his declining years, the reins of power were held by his youngest son, John of Gaunt, duke of Lancaster (1340–99), who was ambitious but largely ineffectual.

STATUTE OF LABOURERS

The Statute of Labourers (1351) was, in the long run, more important than the Magna Carta. Introduced as a response to the shortage of agriculture labourers after the ravages of the Black Death, it was a weapon of the land-owning classes to keep the workers in line. Amendments were subsequently added, making it even more oppressive. Labourers who did not obey or who absconded were branded or whipped, while employers paying more than the pre-plague rate were heavily fined. But it was to no avail. Labourers did move to parts of the country where administration was lax or they went to work in one of the towns with no questions asked. The law of supply and demand inevitably won. Landlords stopped trying to enforce the unenforceable, and labourers were eventually given their own land for which they paid rent. From these labourers came the yeoman farmer, soon to be the backbone of England.

RICHARD II (1377–99)

Edward III was succeeded by his grandson, Richard, the son of Edward, the Black Prince. Richard was only ten years old on his accession, and the country was ruled by his uncles, John of Gaunt and Thomas of Gloucester. There were early problems. The Peasants' Revolt, which broke out in 1381 in response to the imposition of the poll tax and because of widespread anger at low wages and a demand for a review of feudal laws, signalled a new kind of threat. Led by Wat Tyler and John Ball, some 100,000 rebels, burning, looting and murdering as they marched, entered London. The end of their servitude was promised by the fourteen-year-old king,

A portrait of Richard II, the first painting of an English monarch. It indicates the extraordinary progress of the arts, despite the chaos of the time.

who ostentatiously (and bravely) allied himself with the rebels. The promise was not kept, but the land-owners were made even more aware of the power of the peasantry.

There was a rising of discontented nobles in 1387, as ominous to the king and his associates as the massed peasantry, and a group of powerful barons ordered the banishment or killing of the king's friends and advisers. In 1389 Richard took control, and for the next eight years or so he seems to have been a moderate, sensible ruler.

In 1394 he led an army to keep Ireland subdued – a thankless task, for it was received wisdom that occupying powers, including Vikings and Normans, should stay in the coastal regions of Dublin and Cork. He tried again in 1399, but with scant success. The war with France continued, sometimes quiescent, sometimes flaring up.

Richard's wife, Anne of Bohemia, died in 1394, and two years later he married Isabella, the daughter of Charles VI of France. From this point his character began to change, and he had less regard for constitutional government. Richard's uncle and one-time adviser John of Gaunt died in 1399, and Henry, duke of Hereford, surnamed Bolingbroke, who had long been a thorn in the king's side and been exiled in 1397, became duke of Lancaster. Richard hastened back from Ireland, but Bolingbroke had already returned from exile and seized the throne. Richard was imprisoned in Pontefract Castle, where he died in 1400, a rambling depressive, aged only thirty-three. He died of neglect, food, heat and warm clothing having been denied to him.

Fickle and unreliable, Richard II was a connoisseur of the arts, particularly music. He is alleged to have invented the handkerchief, perhaps not a great contribution to English culture. His portrait, displayed in Westminster Abbey, is the earliest known painting of an English monarch. He appears suitably downcast, for his was not a great reign. Centuries later, the tomb was desecrated by boys from Westminster School, one of whom stole a royal rib.

But the fourteenth century, for all the turbulence, marks the time when England became truly England, typified by Geoffrey Chaucer (1340–1400). His *Canterbury Tales*, begun in 1387, opened a window on real life, as Chaucer described everyday events, including the lives of the clerics and their weaknesses as well as the day-to-day business of the common folk. The war with France was far away. It was not the concern of the many.

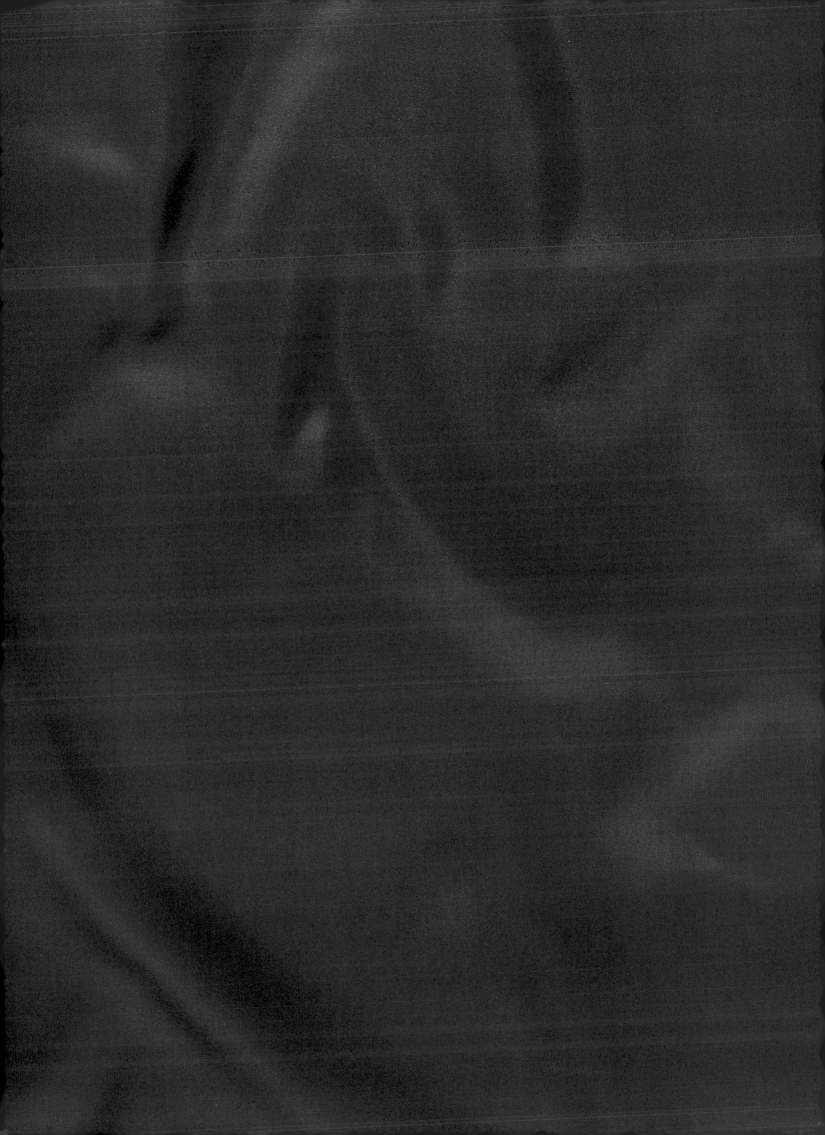

House of Lancaster

On Richard's abdication, the Plantagenets, at odds with one another, divided into the houses of Lancaster and York. Bolingbroke, duke of Lancaster, became king as Henry IV, although there were stronger candidates for the throne. The principle of primogeniture was ignored.

Above: A Parliament of the time, surprisingly informal, perhaps accurate, with a high proportion of clergy, or at least people who look like clergy.

Right: A surprisingly pious view of Henry V.

Unwilling or unable to follow up this victory, Henry V marched to Calais and returned to England. The Genoese, allies of the French and a great sea power, were threatening to control the English Channel. Henry drove them away.

In 1417 he returned to France, vanquished Normandy in three quick campaigns, and in 1420, by the treaty of Troyes, he became heir to the French king and therefore virtually ruler of France. The achievement was illusory. Fighting continued, and Henry's brother Thomas, duke of Clarence, was killed in 1421. Henry returned to France and died there in 1433, his life's ambition of succeeding to the French throne unachieved.

HENRY VI (1422–61; 1470–71)

The new king was Henry V's son, Henry VI, who was less than a year old. John, duke of Bedford, was appointed regent of France, and Humphrey, duke of Gloucester, became regent of England. Gentle, placid and peaceable, Henry VI enjoyed – if that is the right word – a long reign. A devout man, Henry had a passion for education and architecture. King's College, Cambridge (conceived in 1441, eventually completed in 1515), exemplified both his enthusiasms.

In 1429 Joan of Arc instilled a new mood of defiance in France, and the English began to be expelled, although Joan herself was burned at the stake in 1431. But the momentum continued, and 1453 marked the end of the Hundred Years War, with the English all but driven out of France. Henry became mentally ill and Richard, duke of York, Henry's cousin, was appointed Protector. This arrangement lasted a year, when he was dismissed. He promptly rebelled and took over the government following his victory at the battle of St Albans (1455). This was the start of the Wars of the Roses (1455–85) between the Lancastrian and the Yorkist Plantagenets. It was a complicated time. The Protector's son assumed power as Edward IV in 1461, but there was no certainty that he would retain the throne in the face of so many squabbles and conflicts.

The protagonists were many and formidable, not least the belligerent and warlike wife of Henry VI, Margaret of Anjou, who in 1460 raised an army in the north to fight the Yorkists, after the Lancastrians had been defeated by Richard Neville, earl of Warwick, known as the Kingmaker. He could also be described as the Kingbreaker, because he fell out with Edward IV and defeated him at the battle of Edgecote (1469). They were later reconciled, although Warwick, an inherently wise man, but later as treacherous as the rest, was banished. He made peace with Margaret, raised an army, and Edward was forced to fly to Flanders. The pathetic Henry VI was restored to the throne in 1470, but in the following year Edward defeated Margaret's forces at Tewkesbury. The king was captured and murdered in the Tower of London.

Overleaf left: The crowning of Henry VI, curious as he became king at the age of one.

Overleaf right: Henry VI painted by an artist of the school of Francois Clouet (1510-72), retrospective as Henry died in 1471.

The assumption of Henry VI to the throne was a signal for the start of the ill-fated War of the Roses, one faction of the Plantagenets against another. This illustration of Henry in warlike mode exalts him; in reality he was a much less noble figure.

HENRI   VI

House of York

The Wars of the Roses did not effect the increasing prosperity of the country. There were battles fought by the elite, many of whom were killed. A ruling class was being wiped out.

EDWARD IV (1461–70; 1471–83)

Henry VI's death was not the end of the fighting; the fortunes of the warring parties swayed to and fro, but surprisingly it hardly affected the increasing prosperity of the country. Both sides adhered to the policy of "slay the nobles, spare the commons", and both sides avoided rape, pillage and massacre. Although rich in treachery, double-dealing and cold-blooded murder, it was an upper-class war, watched with bemusement by the merchants, the farmers and the common folk. The bloodiest battle – perhaps the most

Edward IV in council. Progressive and enterprising, Edward encouraged overseas trade, dabbling in it himself to renew the state coffers.

bloody fought on English soil – was at Towton in 1461, Contemporary sources state that the armies were each of about 30,000 men each, but in fact they were about half that. Battles were hectic, merciless and often incompetently fought. At the battle of Barnet in 1471 (Edward IV versus his cousin, the earl of Warwick), the armies groped for each other in heavy fog, overlapping without knowing it. One part of one army blundered into another section, thought there was treachery afoot and were routed. The earl of Warwick was cut down and killed.

In the early years and between fighting, Warwick ruled the country while Edward enriched himself in commercial enterprises to bolster the crown and pay off debts, which had been accumulating under Henry VI. There was tension when Edward married Elizabeth Woodville, widow of a commoner, of whom Warwick disapproved. A flawless dynasty was all.

Edward was one of the ablest rulers. He was skilled in commerce, law and diplomacy, and he encouraged trade with Europe by allowing the German Hanseatic League to have privileges. He recognized the contributions of merchant companies and dabbled successfully in the wool and cloth trades, the greatest contributors to English wealth. Irksome as the Wars of the Roses were, they did not interfere with economic progress. Trade boomed, and a new age opened in 1476 with the establishment of William Caxton's first printing press.

Edward could be ruthless. In 1478 a dispute with his brother, George, duke of Clarence, an unpleasant intriguer, ended in Clarence's death in the Tower of London, by drowning, it was said, in a butt of Malmsey wine.

Edward IV could be ruthless. His scheming brother Clarence was drowned in a butt of wine.

THE FIRST PUBLISHER

William Caxton (*c.*1422–*c.*1491) published nearly a hundred books. His industry was prodigious, for he also translated about twenty books. He established the English language, carefully choosing which of the dozens of local dialects to adopt – and these were always changing. Previously, the "popular" language had been the dialect of the west Midlands. Chaucer gave English a London slant. But for him and his like, we would all be speaking a distinctly different language.

Earl Rivers presenting the printer Caxton to Edward IV. Caxton produced the first printing press in England using moveable wooden type in 1476

Above: Edward V one of the princes in the Tower.

Above: The princes in the Tower of London.

Opposite: From all the evidence Richard III was not the hunchbacked creature of Shakespeare's imagination, though this Italian painting of about the sixteenth century perhaps flatters him.

EDWARD V (1483)

Edward IV was only 40 when he died, worn out by fighting and debauchery, and once again the crown passed to a boy, his son, the twelve-year-old Edward V. A Protector was again necessary, and this time it was Edward IV's brother, Richard, duke of Gloucester. Edward V was declared illegitimate, and he became one of the princes in the Tower along with his younger brother, Richard.

No one knows what happened to them. Were they murdered by the duke of Gloucester? Shakespeare thought so, and there is some documentary evidence to support it, for Richard had no qualms in dealing ruthlessly with his enemies, real or imagined.

The last time the princes were seen was in September 1483 in the grounds of the Tower of London. It was five years since their uncle the duke of Clarence had spent his brief spell there.

The way was open to the most notorious of English kings, Richard III.

RICHARD III (1483–85)

Hunch-backed, treacherous, a child-murderer, so obviously evil that the dogs barked at him – this is the popular view of Richard III, largely derived from the character portrayed in Shakespeare's play. There is, however, no evidence that he was deformed – on the contrary, he seems to have been a remarkably handsome man – and there is little evidence of anything untoward about his personality. Richard was in his early thirties when he came to the throne; it was a brief reign, but a lot was crammed into it. The foundation of the College of Arms brought order from chaos, compulsory gifts from individuals to the monarch (benevolences) were abolished, the bail system for accused men and women was introduced, and parliamentary statutes were written down in English for the first time. Richard also promoted education, endowing colleges at Cambridge. These were not the acts of a monster.

Whatever his good points, there is no doubt that suspicions that Richard had had a hand in the disappearance of the princes in the Tower undermined his popularity. In addition, although the succession was theoretically settled, it was still open season for treason, and the duke of Buckingham, a one-time ally, plotted with Henry Tudor, earl of Richmond, the leading Lancastrian contender for the throne. Buckingham was promptly captured and put to death.

In August 1485 Henry Tudor, who had been biding his time in Brittany, landed at Milford Haven in Wales with 3,000 French mercenaries and began to march inland, picking up considerable support as he went.

The royalist forces were under the command of the brothers Lord Thomas and Sir William Stanley. Henry Tudor had 5,000 men; the royalists had 10,000. However, this was largely irrelevant because the Stanley brothers were in communication with Henry Tudor and were waiting for the opportunity to betray the king as he moved from London. Richard, with the small force that remained loyal to him, was killed at Bosworth Field, near Leicester. This battle is often regarded as marking the end of the Wars of the Roses, although minor hostilities continued for several years. Perhaps the most striking feature of the period was that the earls and barons would never again pose such a threat to the monarchy: the Tudors had arrived, and with them came prosperity, peace, the end of civil war – and absolutism.

House of Tudor

Henry VII revived the Court of Star Chamber to discipline any unruly barons who were left. Henry VIII was quite ready to discipline anybody who got in his way, including the pope. Religion became a factor in the succession, to the undying shame of the nation.

Opposite: Henry VII was one of the great kings. The Wars of the Roses had ended, the barons were in disarray, and it was time for harmony. The arts were encouraged, the church was fairly treated, and the sick and the poor were regarded with compassion.

HENRY VII (1485–1509)

Soon after taking power as Henry VII, the new king made certain that rifts were healed by marrying Elizabeth of York, daughter of Edward IV, thus the Yorkists and Lancastrians were united. The Court of Star Chamber was revived to try any barons who broke the law or who raised standing armies. France was invaded yet again, more from habit than from anything else, but Henry was bought off. Military adventures were often undertaken to get money from parliament (whether it was used in war or not) or to blackmail the loser. Italian and French scholars were encouraged to come to England, the church was generously treated, and the sick and the poor were regarded with compassion. Overseas voyages were sponsored, especially that of John and Sebastian Cabot to America in 1497 (Columbus had discovered America in 1492).

Risings against Henry were neither serious nor long-lived. Lambert Simnel (*c.*1477–*c.*1534) posed first as a son of Edward IV and then as Edward, earl of Warwick, the son of the duke of Clarence. He was supported by Margaret of Burgundy and landed in Ireland with 2,000 German mercenaries. He was summarily dismissed, however, and spent his life in the king's service, mostly in the kitchen. Perkin Warbeck (*c.*1474–99) claimed to be Richard, the younger of the princes in the Tower, and he made several attempts to land in England and Ireland, supported by Edward IV's widow, Margaret, and considerable foreign interests. After landing in Kent in 1495, he was captured and later executed.

For a long time England was not under threat. Henry's eldest daughter married James IV of Scotland, while his son, the future Henry VIII, married Catherine of Aragon, thus aligning England with Spain, France's enemy. England seemed ideally placed to move forwards, assuming the leading role in Europe. It was a quiet time, a time for consensus and reconciliation, and of increasing national prosperity. Henry VII had hardly put a step wrong. He died when he was fifty-two.

The Court of the Star Chamber was instituted in 1486 by Henry VII, though its roots are earlier. It was above the law, and was abolished by the Long Parliament in 1641.

HENRY VIII (1509–47)

If Alfred the Great was the embodiment of virtue, Henry V a heroic figure, and Henry VI a pathetic appeaser, Henry VIII (b.1491) was a larger-than-life womanizer with gigantic appetites. The younger son of Henry VII, he became heir to the throne only on the death of Arthur, his elder brother, in 1502. He seems to have had no burning desire to rule, leaving the task to, first, Thomas, later Cardinal, Wolsey (*c.*1475–1530), then Thomas More (1478–1535). Wolsey was accused of high treason but died before he could be brought to trial; More was executed. During Henry VIII's reign at least 17,000 executions were carried out; some say that the figure was much higher, and one authority puts the total at 70,000.

There were few major wars. Wolsey, whatever his personal failings, was a skilled diplomat, whose aim was to hold the balance between Spain and France. The king invaded France in 1512, capturing Tournay and Terouenne. In the following year the Scots were beaten at the battle of Flodden, and king James IV was killed. Artillery was used at Flodden, but much of the battle was hand-to-hand savagery; 10,000 Scots were killed, but English losses were also heavy.

Many English kings had taken mistresses; Henry VIII changed the pattern – he took wives: Catherine of Aragon (in 1509), Anne Boleyn (in 1533; executed 1536), Jane Seymour (in 1536), Anne of Cleves (in 1540), Catherine Howard (in 1540; executed 1542) and Catherine Parr (in 1543). Henry was desperate for a male heir, and he chose to ignore the requirements of the church in his decision to divorce Catherine of Aragon. The king was excommunicated by the pope in 1533. In the following year the Act of Supremacy was passed, making Henry the supreme head of the Church of England. Thomas More's refusal to accept the king, rather than the pope, as the head of the church led to his execution.

Thomas Cromwell began the dissolution of the monasteries in 1535. Their immense wealth and revenues funded Henry's lavish life-style. Many of the coal fields, particularly in Durham and Northumberland, belonged to the church. Henry took these over, and they proved to be a source of great profit.

Henry VIII surrounded by his six wives. It was remarkable that any of them survived him.

The reign saw the first complete translation of the Bible into English in 1535. Henry founded Trinity College, Cambridge, the largest then formed. A mighty navy was built. If Henry VIII did accomplish anything worthwhile, it was in architecture. His forty residences were not necessarily tasteful, but they were imposing. Some, Richmond Palace and Nonsuch Palace, are almost mythical. Whitehall Palace was confiscated from Cardinal Wolsey, who had also built Hampton Court in 1514 (he gave it to the king in 1525 – a noble gesture that did not save him). St James's Palace is perhaps the most agreeable of the palaces.

As reckless in his behaviour as in his expenditure, Henry VIII could have bankrupted the country had he lived any longer. He died in 1547, aged fifty-five, bloated, corpulent and riddled with disease.

Right: Sir Thomas More was only one of the estimated 17,000 people Henry VIII had executed.

REPUTATIONS

It must not be supposed that Sir Thomas More and Cardinal Wolsey were saintly creatures who little deserved execution. In addition to writing *Utopia*, More wrote scurrilous pamphlets against the new Protestant mood in religion. Wolsey was scheming and hypocritical; he started Cardinal's College in Oxford, later renamed Christ's Church, but it was from funds seized from the dissolution of the monasteries.

EDWARD VI (1547–53)

Henry VIII's effort to have a male heir resulted in Edward VI, the son of the king's union with Jane Seymour. He came to the throne when he was nine years old and died at the age of fifteen. Throughout his short life there were two protectors, Edward Seymour, earl of Hertford, the boy king's uncle, promoted to duke of Somerset (*c.*1506–52), and later, John Dudley, earl of Warwick, who created himself duke of Northumberland (1502–53).

An attempt was made immediately Edward gained the crown in 1547 to marry him off to the five-year old Mary, Queen of Scots. When this plan fell through, once again England invaded Scotland. The English forces numbered 16,000, those of the Scots 23,000, but the English had the superiority in cavalry, artillery and arquebusiers (soldiers with matchlock smooth-bore

The fabulous and long-lost Palace at Richmond.

Left: Edward VI, who came to the throne at nine and died at fifteen, gave an opportunity for usurpers and the unscrupulous, whether they were called protectors or not.

firearms anticipating the musket). The English won the battle of Pinkie (1547) and occupied Edinburgh; it was the last formal battle between the national armies of England and Scotland.

Edward VI's reign was almost totally given over to consolidating the new position of the Church of England, which resulted in Thomas Cranmer's prayer book, first issued in 1549 and still used in many churches today. The Catholic mass was made illegal, statues and icons of the old regime were removed, wall paintings were obliterated, and all was accomplished with only Devon and Cornwall in revolt, a rebellion easily put down using German mercenaries. For kingmakers, and especially the duke of Northumberland, succession was now not only a dynastic consideration but also a religious one. Edward was persuaded to nominate Lady Jane Grey, Northumberland's daughter-in-law, as his heir to ensure the triumph of Protestantism.

MARY I (1553–8)

Tuberculosis snatched Edward VI away, and, as the duke of Northumberland had sought to guarantee, Lady Jane Grey was proclaimed queen, a state of affairs that lasted nine days. Mary (b.1516), daughter of Henry VIII and Catherine of Aragon, advanced on London without bloodshed – indeed, she was welcomed by the populace – and claimed the throne, vowing to restore the Catholic faith. Northumberland was executed, and a year later in 1554 Mary announced her intention of marrying Philip II, king of Spain

Above: Philip of England and Spain. His union with Queen Mary was brief and cold, and he only spent one year in England.

Right: Queen Mary, who brought Roman Catholicism back to England, glorying in her cruelty. Those who refused to forsake Protestantism were burned at the stake.

(1556–98). The union of the two great powers may have been welcome by some, but Sir Thomas Wyatt was aghast at the prospect, and he led a revolt, which was crushed. Wyatt was executed, along with Lady Jane Grey and her husband. The future Queen Elizabeth, Mary's half-sister, was suspected of complicity and was imprisoned in the Tower of London.

Mary, known as Bloody Mary, did marry Philip, although there was no heir. He lived in England for only a year before returning to Spain. Mary, who had remained true to the Church of Rome throughout her brother's reign, began to bring back the old religion. The persecution of the Protestants began, heresy laws were revived, bishops, including the former archbishop of Canterbury, Thomas Cranmer (1489–1556), were burned at the stake, and the new religious order seemed to have been a brief aberration. As a child, Mary had been humiliated and degraded by her refusal to renounce Catholicism; as a woman this was reinforced by an innate pessimism and sourness, anger and despair at her husband's cold-heartedness, and the conviction that the religious savagery she promoted was worthwhile for the sake of Catholicism. It is impossible to say how many heretics were burned at the stake; a likely figure is 300.

During her brief reign – she was only forty-two when she died – religion dominated her life, except for an ill-starred war against France in 1557 in which Calais, the last bastion of English rule on French soil was lost.

ELIZABETH I (1558–1603)

Somewhat surprisingly there was no struggle for the succession. Perhaps the English people had lost their taste for blood-letting. Elizabeth I, an assured young woman in her mid-twenties, was no innocent in an anarchic world. The switch back to Protestantism was uncompromising, and she chose her advisers well – William Cecil, one of England's greatest statesmen, served her with distinction for forty years. Red-headed, said to be handsome (although her portraits are no guide), proud, wise and tolerant (to a point) – all qualities have been heaped on Elizabeth. She could be ruthless when she had a mind to it, and favourites, such as the earl of Essex, who presumed too much, were executed.

The queen was also pragmatic. Mary, Queen of Scots, the daughter of James V of Scotland, was a great-granddaughter of Henry VII and a possible threat with a credible claim to the English throne. Beautiful, intelligent and well-educated, Mary was, to say the least, unfortunate in her choice of hus-

The ill-fated Lady Jane Grey walking to her execution on a cold February day in 1554. She was only 17 years old.

Left: A marvellous evocation by Frank Moss Bennett (1874-1953) of the court of Queen Elizabeth I.

Above: Mary, Queen of Scots, had the credentials to rule, but Elizabeth was no stranger to butchery when her power was threatened, and Mary was executed.

Left: Sir Francis Drake, pirate, hero, one of the great characters thrown up by this expansive and confident period.

bands. She was also a Catholic. First married to the dauphin (later François II), on his death in 1561 she returned to Scotland and married her cousin, the earl of Darnley. After being implicated in the murder of Rizzio, Mary's secretary, Darnley was himself murdered in 1567 in a conspiracy organized by the earl of Bothwell, whom Mary soon married. A rebellion broke out and Mary was imprisoned, but she escaped and fled to England, where she threw herself on the mercy of her cousin, Elizabeth. The queen prevaricated, but, following the Babington plot and fearful of a Catholic uprising, she agreed that Mary should be put on trial and, in 1587, that she should be executed.

It was an age of adventure, massive trade expansion, innovation and invention, and it would have been so without the queen. But she encouraged it, though reining in her more dashing subjects when their ventures tended to become out of hand. Slave-trading with America, the encouragement of Sir Francis Drake and his piracy, and the sponsorship of Sir Walter Raleigh and his historic voyages of discovery — Elizabeth was involved in them all. She knew when to act, when to refuse to act and when to delegate. The defeat of the Spanish Armada in 1588 was a triumph of self-confidence and single-mindedness.

There was little compassion for the poor — the Poor Law (1601) taxed property owners, to their chagrin, but the poor had no place in the grand pattern. The arts bloomed as never before, with music, literature, painting and architecture achieving new heights. Between 1530 and 1600 the population of London increased from 50,000 to over 200,000. Between 1580 and 1594, in an early example of civic enterprise, lead pipes were installed to bring water from the Thames. It was a golden age, marred only by the plague of 1563–4 in which over 20,000 people died in London alone, some probably through drinking polluted water from the Thames.

Above: Shakespeare mirrored the age of Elizabeth as no other person could.

Opposite: Elizabeth I was regarded as a handsome woman even though she had to wear a wig in later life. She was a dignified and forceful monarch, reigning until in her seventieth year, longer than any of her predecessors.

House of Stuart

The Stuarts brought style into the monarchy, and encouraged the arts and architecture. They were also hot-headed, and were inclined to take a cavalier attitude towards parliament. Parliament rebelled, and England became a republic. The Commonwealth and the Protectorate interrupted the legal procession for a few traumatic years.

JAMES I (1603–25)

Having never married, Elizabeth had no one to succeed her, and there was no obvious natural heir. King James VI of Scotland (b.1566) was the son of Mary, Queen of Scots and Lord Darnley; he was also the great-grandson of Henry VIII's sister, Margaret Tudor, the wife of James IV. In 1603 he became James I of England and remained James VI of Scotland, thus uniting the two countries and becoming the first of the Stuarts (formerly Stewarts). Vain, suspicious and cruel, with curious eccentricities, he was well-educated but lacked perception: "the wisest fool in Christendom," according to Erasmus. He promoted the Authorized Version of the Bible (published in 1611) and arranged a well-regulated peace with Spain, perhaps his greatest triumph, for without it Spain could well have become the natural enemy instead of France.

As far as the nobles were concerned, the king's Protestantism was welcome, but his attitude to Catholicism seems to have been ambivalent. The Catholics had gone under cover during the reign of Elizabeth, but they briefly emerged to try to blow up the king, his ministers and both houses of parliament in the Gunpowder Plot of 1605. Guy Fawkes was discovered with the gunpowder in the cellar of the Palace of Westminster, underwent torture for months with the full approval of the king and was finally hanged, drawn and quartered. It is believed by some that the Gunpowder Plot was hatched up by the ruling faction to discredit Catholics and thus give credence to those who wanted to hound them to death in revenge for the Marian persecutions.

Despite his evident faults, James patronized the arts, encouraging the great architect Inigo Jones who designed the Queen's House at Greenwich (completed in the 1630s) and his masterpiece, the Banqueting House in Whitehall (1619). He commissioned portraiture by the leading Flemish artists of the time. There were no great wars in his twenty-two-year reign, and a flare-up in Ireland was dealt with easily, although pacifying the country was always temporary.

Above: Anne of Denmark was the queen of James I. Her main claim to fame is that she was six foot seven inches tall.

Right: The conspirators of the Gunpowder Plot, Catholics determined to blow up King James I. The leader, Guy Fawkes, underwent terrible torture for months on end.

Opposite: James I of England (and concurrently James VI of Scotland) was the great-grandson of Henry VIII's sister, so his claim to the throne, though valid, was hardly by direct descent. He was the first of the Stuart (formerly Stewart) dynasty.

Jacob · der · Konnig · Sechst · Ko · von Schottlandi ·

WESTMINSTER BURIALS

The dean of Westminster, Arthur Stanley (1815–81), made it his business to find out exactly where the monarchs' bodies were buried in Westminster Abbey. At first he could not find James I, but he persevered and eventually discovered the tomb alongside that of Henry VII. James I hated smoking, and wrote a virulent attack on the obnoxious habit. By the side of his coffin Stanley found a clay pipe, left by some workman in the past.

CHARLES I (1625–49)

James I's eldest son, Henry, had died in 1612, and the throne passed to his second son, Charles. James I had been impatient of parliament, failing to see its relevance, and Charles I was even more forthright, dissolving it in 1626, a year after he became king, when it attempted to impeach his favourite, the libertine George Villiers, duke of Buckingham (the first duke not of royal blood).

Prince Rupert, the German-born nephew of Charles I, was the victor over the Parliamentarians at the Battle of Edgehill. It was a short respite for the monarch.

Opposite: Charles I was a cultured man, shy yet arrogant, and he treated Parliament with scant respect, dissolving it at will, and paving the way for the revolution. He is shown here with a hunting party.

Opposite: Charles II brought European values and culture to an England becoming anchored in the past. During his reign the country thrived, despite the natural disasters of the Great Plague and the Great Fire of London a year afterwards.

PUNISHMENT OF SIN

If the laws that existed in Cromwell's time were enforced today a large proportion of the population would be dead. In 1650 an act was passed punishing adultery with death; this penalty was enforced in two or three cases, but even Puritan juries were reluctant to convict. Church courts had existed to punish sin, and the penalty for adultery or fornication was to stand in public wearing a white sheet. Cromwell, however, thought it was the state's business, not that of the church. After Cromwell's time punishment for "sin" judicially lapsed, except for homosexuality, which could be a capital offence. Lesbianism was never a crime, as no one dared to explain to Queen Victoria what it was.

CHARLES II (1660–85)

In 1660 parliament invited Charles I's eldest son, Charles (b.1630) to return. Oliver Cromwell, buried in Westminster Abbey, was dug up and put on display. It was an uncharacteristic move, for Charles II was an open-minded man. He was inclined to scepticism, and was a libertine with a string of mistresses, often two at a time, including the great and noble as well as the

Below: The arrival of Charles II from abroad was dramatic but inevitable. The country was not ready to be a republic, and the power and potential threat of the New Model Army was only too obvious.

Right: The Great Plague of 1665, brought in by rats, which killed 100,000 people in London alone.

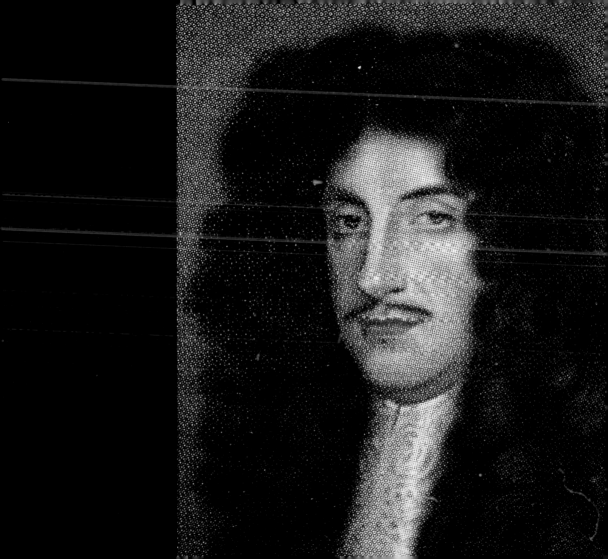

actress Nell Gwynne. He encouraged the arts, promoted science, which was forging ahead at a tremendous rate, by inaugurating the Royal Society, and brought back from Europe a sophistication not known in England. He bore down, but not brutally, on Puritanism and Nonconformity, and throughout his reign pursued financially damaging wars with the Dutch. He was also cunning; by promising to become a Catholic and restore Catholicism in England he received secret subsidies from Louis XIV of France.

Immensely popular among all classes, he had passed the Habeas Corpus Act (1679), protecting individuals from arbitrary arrest. There were natural disasters – bubonic plague in 1665, which killed more than 100,000 people in London alone; and the Great Fire of London in 1666, which destroyed 440 acres and more than 13,000 buildings. This disaster cleared the way for Sir Christopher Wren to rebuild more than fifty churches, including St Paul's Cathedral, converting London from a medieval town to a capital city.

JAMES II (1685–88)

Charles II died in 1685 at the age of fifty-four, and his brother James, Charles's second son, became king. He was a Catholic, and dissent was inevitable. An attempt to put Charles's illegitimate son, the duke of Monmouth, on the throne was thwarted. Monmouth himself, who had landed in Dorset with eighty-two men but who built up a considerable

James II receiving the news that William of Orange had landed and was ready to grasp the throne.

following, was defeated at the battle of Sedgemoor (1685), captured, tried and executed. This was the last battle on English soil. James II made certain such impertinence would not happen again; Judge Jeffreys, a willing tool of the crown, managed the Bloody Assizes – 331 of Monmouth's followers were hanged, 849 were despatched to the American colonies, thirty-three were fined or whipped.

In 1686 James II stationed an army at Hounslow near London in case the Londoners refused to embrace the Catholic faith, and all acts of parliament against Catholics and Nonconformists were revoked. Yet during his reign there was a great influx of Huguenots (French Protestants), from France who settled in England following the revocation of the Edict of Nantes in 1685. The Huguenots brought valuable skills – they started the silk industry in Spitalfields, and many were skilled gold- and silversmiths.

The birth of a son to James in 1688 was the signal that the Catholic regime would be perpetuated, and seven leading statesmen invited the Protestant William of Orange, the stadtholder of the United Netherlands, to take the throne. William was the son of Charles II's eldest daughter, Mary, and William II of Holland. In 1688 William disembarked at Brixham in Devon – the invasion fleet numbered 200 transports and fifty warships – and marched on London, picking up support on the way. James fled, as did Judge Jeffreys disguised as a sailor, but he was apprehended at Wapping and sent to

Below: The task of dealing with the aftermath of the rebellion was given to Judge Jeffreys. The Bloody Assizes remains a blot on English law to this day.

Left: James II was Charles's second son, a Catholic, and an attempt to put Charles II's illegitimate son the Duke of Monmouth on the throne was bloodily put down.

Above: King William III and his wife Mary, daughter of James II, accepting the English throne. Like Charles II, he brought continental ideas, and fostered culture and economic advancement, though his shyness and foreign ideas were not greatly liked by his subjects.

Below: The Duke of Marlborough, the victor of the Battle of Blenheim, and a distant ancestor of Sir Winston Churchill.

Opposite: Queen Anne came to the throne in 1702.

the Tower of London, where died four months later, lamented by none.
James II fled to France.

WILLIAM AND MARY (1689–1702)

The deposition of James II and the invitation to Mary, the eldest daughter of James II, and her husband William, are known as the Glorious Revolution. The new monarchs accepted a new constitutional settlement, the Bill of Rights (1689), which assured the superiority of parliamentary rule over monarchical powers.

William III had been a fine soldier, and he continued inconclusive wars in Europe. James's supporters landed in Londonderry in Ireland, and William fought and won the battle of the Boyne (1690), an event that created a rift that exists to this day between Catholics and Protestants in Ireland.

William III was never popular with his English subjects, but he was a brilliant statesman, adroitly managing a grand alliance between England, Holland and Austria (1701) that prevented a potential union of France and Spain, the potential superpower. This led to the War of Spanish Succession.

His reign was full of landmarks – the National Debt was started, the Bank of England established, Lloyds of London began, there was religious toleration, and he introduced Dutch architecture to England. In 1695 press censorship was abolished. As with Charles II, he also brought continental ideas, making England less insular. There were parliamentary changes, and the reign saw the beginning of the more efficient cabinet government. Mary died in 1694, and William ruled alone. In 1702, while he was out riding, his horse stumbled on a mole-hill, and he fell and died. Although he ruled for less than thirteen years, his influence on the life and times of England and English society was considerable and is inclined to be under-valued.

ANNE (1702–14)

Queen Anne was the second daughter of James II and sister-in-law of William III. She came to the throne in 1702, a woman of thirty-seven, already worn out by continual pregnancies. She had seventeen children by her husband George, Prince of Denmark, only one of whom survived infancy, and he died at the age of twelve.

It was a reign of scientific and intellectual progress, the first daily newspaper appeared in London (*The Daily Courant*), literature and the arts flourished, fine, elegant furniture was made and even formal sporting events were arranged with the establishment of horse racing at Ascot. And there were great wars. The battle of Blenheim (1704), largely won by John Churchill, duke of Marlborough and fought against the French and her allies, involved armies totalling 116,000 men. Marlborough was later removed from command for using army money for his own use, but not before Blenheim Palace, his reward for his achievement, was given to him (though it was not completed until 1722, the year of his death).

Victory at Blenheim made England a great continental power, and the War of the Spanish Succession was ended with the signing of the treaty of Utrecht in 1713 by England and France.

The Act of Union of 1707 closely united England with Scotland, which lost its parliament. There was religious tolerance. Few people were persecuted, and the last execution for witchcraft in England took place in 1712, although it remained a crime until 1736. As late as 1863 a man accused for being a wizard was ducked and died.

House of Hanover

During the Hanoverian period the monarchy became marginalized. The Georges were essentially foreigners, and made little attempt to interfere with Robert Walpole and his successors, and policies were made by ministers. Internal dissent was almost nil; the efforts of the Old Pretender and the Young Pretender were always destined to fail. It was the age of enlightenment, and the age of the Industrial Revolution which transformed not only Britain but the rest of the world. Queen Victoria, perhaps the best of all monarchs, reversed the trend of monarchy, playing a key part in the governing of the country.

In disguise, the Young Pretender fled, helped by Flora MacDonald. He died in poverty in Rome in 1788, a sad embittered man.

Cumberland earned the sobriquet of "Butcher" for his ruthlessness. Of 1,000 Scottish prisoners, most were killed out of hand. The Scottish culture was suppressed, clan chiefs were ignominiously stripped of their authority, and a price was put on Charles Stuart's head. Dressed in woman's clothing, he tried to avoid capture with the help of Flora MacDonald. Supporters were now hard to find, for the Scots were demoralized. Charles found exile in France, and died in poverty in Rome in 1788.

It was the end of one age but the beginning of another. By 1760, when George II died, British influence had begun to stretch around the world, from settlements in the Gambia and on the Gold Coast of Africa, to Bermuda and other West Indian and Caribbean islands, to Canada, and, of course, to India.

THE BRITISH ARMY

The first truly professional army in England was Cromwell's "New Model Army". It was almost the last. The Duke of Wellington described the rank and file in his victorious armies as "the scum of the earth", adding: "It is really wonderful we should have made them the fine fellows they are." The principal causes for enlistment were drink, unemployment, or trouble with a woman or the law. Discipline was harsh; Field Punishment Number One, being tied to a gun-carriage and flogged, could be fatal.

GEORGE III (1760–1820)

George III was the grandson of George II, his father, Frederick Louis, having predeceased him. England needed good government and advisers, and in George III the nation had a sterling king. Unusually, he had a happy, secure marriage to Charlotte Sophia. He was religious without being censorious of others, hard-working and so engrossed in the science of agriculture (at which he was expert) that he was known as Farmer George.

His first prime minister, the earl of Bute, was an incompetent, and some of the others were hardly better. The attempt to impose tax on the American colonies resulted in the Boston Tea Party in 1773, the War of Independence in 1776 and the loss of America. These events proved to be immensely important, but they were only casually regarded at the time.

In 1771 *Encyclopaedia Britannica* was first published; accurate informed knowledge, for almost the first time in England, was widely available by turning the pages of a book. In 1773 the first cast-iron bridge was erected at Coalbrookdale. It is still there, a monument to engineering and the coming age. John Smeaton's water-wheels transformed the use of water power. James Watt's steam engine revolutionized the use of power itself, and shaped the future of the country, proving to be far more important in the long run than James Cook's first voyage around the world or the publishing of great but unread books such as Thomas Paine's *The Rights of Man* (1791–92).

In 1788 an event of great sadness occurred. George III had his first attack of madness, now known to be the hereditary disease porphyria. Openly regarded as comical (hospitals for the insane were widely regarded as amusement centres), the illness surfaced at periods, causing his wife to drift away from him, and she encouraged the doctors in ill-advised and bizarre new treatments for her husband.

Opposite: King George III, known as "Farmer George" because of his all-abiding interest in agriculture. Stable and conscientious, he presided over the Industrial Revolution without being too aware of it.

Opposite: The vainglorious spendthrift King George IV, who was everything his father George III was not.

DUELLING

Of all the occupations that marked the status of a gentleman, duelling occupies prime place. It served the purpose of a knightly joust. Duels in the eighteenth century had been fought with rapiers; in the nineteenth century pistols were the preferred weapon. In 1829 the duke of Wellington, then prime minister, "called out" Lord Winchilsea. Fortunately he did not kill him.

WILLIAM IV (1830–37)

William IV ascended the throne in 1830, much to his surprise. He was George III's third son, but his elder brother, the Duke of York, had died in 1827. William IV was sixty-four, a one-time naval man, who was noted for his tactlessness and lack of style, thus his nickname "Silly Billy". He was also friendly and approachable. He had married late in life and his only children were illegitimate – ten of them by the actress Mrs Dorothy Jordan. His

King William IV, "Silly Billy", reigned for only a short time. His influence on the nation was negligible.

great asset was that he did not interfere. Parliament passed acts that determined the future of the country; the Reform Act of 1832 gave half a million more men the vote, and seats in parliament were distributed more evenly, so that booming industrial towns and cities acquired members of parliament for the first time.

Although slavery was abolished throughout the British Empire (1833) and children under nine were forbidden to work in factories (an act often ignored and impossible to uphold), the "Tolpuddle Martyrs" were sentenced to seven years' transportation for attempting to organize a trade union, and the Poor Law Amendment Act (1834) provided workhouses, separating husbands from wives and forcing hard and menial labour on them. It was perhaps a good thing that the same year the Houses of Parliament were burned down. Britain, wealthy and grand, had an increasingly seamy side, explored by Charles Dickens in *Oliver Twist* (1837), the year that William IV died. Perhaps it was a pity that he did not intervene more.

CRUEL SPORTS

Sport in the early nineteenth century was crude, cruel and savage. Gradually the worst excesses were curbed. Bullbaiting was made illegal in 1835, and cockfighting was prohibited in 1849 (although it went underground and is still practised). Bare-knuckle fighting (prize fighting) was probably the most popular sport during the Regency period, and even aristocrats took lessons from the masters. Horse-racing retained general respect, thanks largely to the powerful jurisdiction of the Jockey Club, which was established in 1750.

Victoria and her loving consort, Prince Albert, made Scotland fashionable. She had no compunctions about taking the new-fangled train; she was also later one of the first people to have a telephone.

VICTORIA (1837–1901)

Queen Victoria was William's niece. Obstinate, determined, compassionate
and highly intelligent, she was eighteen years old on her accession, and
she was mistakenly regarded as an inexperienced girl who could be manip-
ulated. She was fortunate in her ministers. Lord Melbourne, cynical and
detached, acted almost as an amiable uncle. Robert Peel was stiff but
incorruptible, and later, in their own ways, Disraeli and Gladstone were
remarkable prime ministers. The rumbling of the masses, especially in the
Chartist movement of 1838–50, was initially alarming, but it was quelled
without bloodshed.

It was a new age, proceeding at an alarming pace. The development of new technology was breathtaking. Domestic appliances and other innovations that we take for granted today – the postal system, the sewing-machine, the typewriter, the telephone – were all introduced, transforming the way people acted, thought and communicated. Late in the reign the automobile made its appearance. Sir Charles Babbage constructed the first (mechanical) computer. Most important of all, the capabilities of electricity were seen and used.

There were tragedies, often badly dealt with, such as the great potato famine in Ireland in 1845–88, and continual outbreaks of cholera in London. Crime was rife, although many petty crimes, such as theft, no longer carried the death penalty. The city slums were worse than anything in medieval England, but attempts were made to deal with them, including the building of model housing for the workers. There were numerous charitable organizations providing the safety net for the most vulnerable.

In 1840 Victoria married Prince Albert of Saxe-Coburg-Gotha (the dynasty was renamed Windsor in World War I as a sop to anti-German feeling), and he was, in the eyes of some, the best king Britain never had. Prince Albert organized perhaps the most noteworthy spectacle of the age, the Great Exhibition of 1851, when 17,000 exhibitors displayed their wares under 19 acres of glass to nearly seven million visitors. Albert died suddenly in 1861, and Victoria was devastated. She withdrew from public duties and entered into a long mourning during which the people began to turn against her. She was persuaded, largely by Disraeli, to resume her public role and she ended her reign in triumph.

There was just one major war during her reign, the Crimean War (1853–56), during which Britain, France, Turkey and Sardinia were allied against Russia. The war was mismanaged and wholly unnecessary, but it made a heroine of Florence Nightingale. Towards the end of Victoria's reign the South African (Boer) War (1899–1902) broke out. There was no doubt about its outcome, but it emphasized the defects of the British military machine and made heroes of men who were to prove criminally incompetent in World War I.

But it was a great reign. The Reform Bill of 1867 made two million men (but no women) eligible to vote. The formation of trades unions was legalized, and the Independent Labour Party was founded by Keir Hardie in 1893. There were problems, too, and what became known as the Irish Problem admitted of no solution. There were assassinations and civil unrest by what were known as the Fenians, creating internal tensions that threatened the very stability of the nation.

No monarch had worked harder than Victoria; no monarch had played such a part in the evolution of a nation; and no monarch had been so self-confident. Large portions of the map of the world were coloured red, the colour of the British Empire. But things were not as they seemed; in industrial production the United States was eclipsing Britain, the Germans were progressing at a fantastic rate, and Britain was resting complacently on its laurels.

House of Saxe-Coburg
Edward VII (1901–10)

Victoria had lived so long that when her son Edward (b.1841) came to the throne in 1901 he was approaching sixty. As the Prince of Wales he had been feckless, a gambler, a womanizer, immensely popular with all classes ("Good Old Teddy") and an invaluable ambassador for British interests abroad. But Queen Victoria, distrusting his judgement, kept him from important duties, a tragic mistake, as he proved to be a good king, at ease with other European monarchs, and paving the way for the Entente Cordiale with France. It was thought that this would counter the threat from an increasingly belligerent Germany, which was building up a navy that would rival the increasingly old-fashioned Royal Navy. Desperately, the navy was re-organized. The invention of the Dreadnought class, the ultimate in warships, rendered every other warship in the world old-fashioned, including the other ships of the Royal Navy.

It was an age that saw the first air flight (by the Wright brothers in 1903), the increasing efficiency and availability of the automobile, and, in 1909, the introduction of the old age pension, the precursor of the welfare state.

Above: Sarah Bernhardt, the actress, one of the many mistresses of Edward VII.

Left: King Edward VII in his coronation regalia. Had he assumed the throne when he was younger, the world may have been a different place.

House of Windsor

During World War I the name of the reigning dynasty was changed to allow for anti-German feeling, and Windsor was a good choice, though there are no dynastic reasons for it being chosen. George V, George VI and Elizabeth II have been exemplary monarchs at a time when monarchy throughout the world has been threatened or has disappeared. Perhaps the institution of monarchy is an anachronism. In a time scale stretching back more than a thousand years it is impossible to tell.

Opposite: King George V and Queen Mary in 1914, popular monarchs, dignified and resolute.

GEORGE V (1910–36)

In 1910 Edward VII died, and his second son, George, came to the throne. Albert Victor, known as Eddy, the eldest son, had died in 1892. George V was dignified, a good man in every way, but he did not interfere. His favourite hobby was philately, but unfortunately stamp collecting was of little help in avoiding the collapse into a war that no one wanted and that brought ruin to Europe. It lasted four years (1914–18) and would have lasted longer had the United States not entered the war. The Irish rebelled and were crushed in 1916, but in 1920–1 the country was partitioned and the Irish Free State was formed in the south.

Popular if a trifle remote, the king's "hands-off" approach to life was not unwelcome. The first Labour government was formed in 1924, the General Strike of 1926 damaged the country (although not as much as the Great Depression afflicted the United States), women over the age of twenty-one got the vote in 1928, and great wealth went alongside great poverty. People starved despite the help given to the needy, while individualism and selfishness were rampant. Lloyd George had promised to "make Britain a fit country for heroes to live in", but this was not to be. In 1935 George V and his strict, uncompromising wife, Mary (1867–1953), held their Silver Jubilee. There were great celebrations, but he was a remote figure to Britain's millions. A year later he died.

George V in army uniform during World War I.

King Edward VIII with his abdication speech, inevitable considering the odium attached in 1936 to marrying Mrs Wallis Simpson, an American divorcee.

EDWARD VIII (1936)

George V's son Edward VIII came to the throne, reigning for less than a year in 1936. As Prince of Wales he had been a popular figure, having an apparently easy rapport with the masses. His determination to marry Mrs Wallis Simpson, a twice-divorced American woman, led to his abdication.

During World War II (1939–1945) the pro-Nazi sympathies of the duke of Windsor, as he became, were something of a liability, and he was unceremoniously despatched to be governor of the Bahamas, where he could do little harm. He died in his adopted country, France, in 1972, aged seventy-seven.

During World War I women took over, efficiently and uncomplainingly, many of the tasks that had hitherto been regarded as men's work. Without effort, they achieved what the women's suffrage movement had never been able to accomplish – the acceptance of women as people in their own right. The results were far-reaching. Their experiences in factories and offices and on the land made women independent. Before the war, many had been in domestic service; after the war, most vowed they would never return to the subservience and humiliation involved, and in the 1920s and 1930s the upper classes had to manage increasingly without servants. This, in turn, gave impetus to the development of labour-saving domestic appliances, including the electric iron, cooker and vacuum cleaner.

The coronation of King George VI in the magnificent setting of Westminster Abbey. Together with his much loved wife, now Queen Elizabeth the Queen Mother, George overcame his initial shyness to become a sterling monarch, respected throughout the world.

GEORGE VI (1936–52)

No one could be less like Edward VIII than his younger brother, George (b.1895), who was suddenly elevated to the throne as George VI in 1936. Shy, diffident and with a terrible stammer, he determined to do his best, and he did. He had fought in the battle of Jutland in World War I (the only major sea battle of the war) and during World War II (1939–45) he remained in London, despite the bombing. Buckingham Palace was itself bombed. He and his consort, Elizabeth, became popular figures, restoring the reputation of the monarchy after the short reign of Edward VIII. George VI died of lung cancer aged fifty-six.

ELIZABETH II (1952–)

Elizabeth II was twenty-five years old when she suddenly became queen. As a child she was grave, reserved and sensible. As a woman she has been a flawless monarch with her consort Prince Philip, whom she married in 1947. Her reign has seen a revolution as great as the one that took place in that of her great-grandmother, Queen Victoria, a revolution that has yet to be evaluated. Like Queen Victoria, she has become deeply involved with the country, its prosperity and its problems; like Queen Victoria, she has had problems with her offspring.

In 1969 she broke with precedent by allowing the British Broadcasting Corporation to make a documentary about the private life of the monarchy, *The Royal Family*. Many commentators think, with hindsight, that this was a mistake, democratizing the undemocratic and removing the mystery from an ancient order more than a thousand years old. It was a further step in giving the people not what they should have, but what they wanted. And the people were not the unquestioningly obedient subjects they once were, divided into the upper, middle and working classes. Ostensibly classless, multi-ethnic, with every nation of the world contributing its share towards a country that has slid down the ranks into a state in the middle range, Britain shares the fate of all the great powers of the past – Norway and Denmark, home of the Vikings, Ireland, whose Celts were feared across Europe, Holland, once the great sea-power challenging England for supremacy, Sweden, whose armies ranged through Europe, Spain, whose empire was incomparably rich, and Portugal, the capital of which, Lisbon, was once the richest city in the world.

In the seesaw of history, Britain retains its Commonwealth, a loose some-times haphazard arrangement of one-time components of the British Empire. Queen Elizabeth II has retained her faith in the Commonwealth. Often, though not always, the Commonwealth has retained its faith in her, as has the great proportion of her subjects. The role of the monarchy has changed, but the monarchy itself, "The Family Firm", is irreplaceable. And woe to anyone who tries to change it.

Opposite: Queen Elizabeth II as painted by Pietro Annigoni in 1954.

Left: HRH Prince Philip, the Duke of Edinburgh.

AFTERWORD
CHARLES &
DIANA

For one brief moment on the morning of August 31st 1997 it seemed as if the earth stood still, frozen in a paroxysm of disbelief. Diana, Princess of Wales had been killed in a car crash in a Paris underpass. The news stunned people the world over. Probably not since the death of the American President, John F. Kennedy in 1963, had the death of one person had such a profound effect.

Her funeral at London's Westminster Abbey a week later on September 6th drew some of the biggest crowds the capital has ever seen. Millions watched on television as the whole nation - and the world - became united in a quite extraordinary outpouring of grief.

Since marrying Charles, Prince of Wales, heir to the British throne, Diana had become, quite simply, the most famous woman in the world. In 1982 she gave birth to Prince William and two years later Prince Harry was born. The line was secure. But sadly her marriage to Prince Charles proved to be anything but.

It had all started so well, with a fairy tale wedding in St Paul's Cathedral on July 29th 1981. It was the most glamorous and spectacular wedding the world had ever seen, attended by 21 sovereigns; 20 heads of state; 26 governors general; countless royals; aristocrats; politicians; friends and a then unknown face in the congregation, Mrs Camilla Parker Bowles.

Charles and Diana spent the main part of their honeymoon on the royal yacht *Britannia*, cruising the Greek islands. On returning they began the endless round of public engagements which is always the lot of the British Royal Family. The people of Britain - and the wider world - took Diana into their hearts and, for the first time in his life, Prince Charles found himself being upstaged. It was not an experience he appeared to enjoy.

The birth of two sons within two years of each other brought much joy to Diana and she poured her heart and soul into ensuring they had a happy and fulfilling upbringing. But as time went by her marriage took on a darker aspect as she began to suspect that her husband, Prince Charles, had rekindled his relationship with an old girlfriend, Camilla Parker Bowles, married at the time to Andrew Parker Bowles, himself a friend of the Prince.

From then it was downhill all the way. Charles and Diana drifted steadily apart; their few public appearances together served only to emphasise the deterioration in their marriage.

On December 9th 1992 it was announced that they had formally separated. Their divorce took place on August 28th 1996. A year later Diana was dead.

At the time the Prince of Wales was deeply unpopular with the public at large. It was felt he had misused his beautiful, young and trusting wife and cheapened his position as heir to the throne. Since then opinion has slowly drifted his way again,

Above: A pensive looking Prince Charles on yet another overseas tour, this time the Cameroons.

Opposite: Sealed with a kiss – Prince Charles and his new bride on the balcony of Buckingham Palace following the wedding ceremony. They were joined by various members of the Royal Family, including Queen Elizabeth II.

Below: Diana seemed always at her most relaxed when she was with her children, as shown here with a young Prince Harry on a trip to Spain in August 1987.

helped no doubt by his obvious and genuine love for his two sons.

Prince Charles was born in 1948 and is now in his 50s. His mother, Queen Elizabeth II was only 26 when she inherited the throne. There are inevitable comparisons to be made with Queen Victoria and her son Edward VII who did not become king until he was 59, reigning for only nine years.

But whenever Prince Charles does ascend the throne, all the signs are that he will make an excellent king. He is a sensitive, well educated and well rounded person who is deeply committed to the welfare of others. He has a passion for the environment, music and the arts and, above all, has a deep love for his country and its people, whatever their race or creed.

Left: A smiling Prince William on his first day at Eton, probably the most famous public school in Britain.

Opposite: Charles and Diana in happier times before they were married, relaxing within the beautiful and extensive grounds of Balmoral in Scotland.

Index

Picture Credits